The Prematurely Saved

for Regina

The Prematurely
Saved And Other Varieties
of the Religious Experience

* * * * * * * * * * * * * * *

Templegate Publishers/Springfield, Illinois

ISBN:0-87243-150-9

Printed in the United States of America

The essays in this collection were, for the most part, published first in *Commonweal*. "Some Difficulties of Modern Spirituality" first appeared in *Communio*. "Orthodoxy: the Third Way" first appeared in the *Critic*. The author and publishers thank the editors of each of these journals for permission to reprint.

Published by
Templegate Publishers
302 East Adams St.
Springfield, IL 62701

TABLE OF CONTENTS

Introduction

Any writer, no matter what he might say about it, believes in one part of his soul that almost anything he writes is worthy of collection and a permanent place on somebody's shelf. It is true that notices of books long forgotten, commentary on obscure regional elections, and reviews of cancelled television series are probably an exception; but then, the writer thinks (making a grandiose comparison) there was Orwell, whose reviews are still worth reading long after their subjects have faded.

Writers believe this in theory, and then are shocked when an honest look back reveals that the review which once looked good is now faded and dull beyond belief, and the turn of phrase which once seemed so sparkling is revealed in the morning light to be a cheap and self-satisfying jab. When the publishers first brought up the possibility of this collection I was pleased. At last all of those columns and reviews would have a place to rest—a deserved place, at that. But so many were dated; all the references to President Carter or to old television movies and pop stars were hopelessly time-bound. Some of the writing was best buried and forgotten. It was a humbling experience.

Some things held up, though, and I saw themes which mattered to me taken up repeatedly in ways which expanded them as a single and sustained essay could not. Not everything was hopeless in all the stuff I had turned out against deadline, and although I might now find this paragraph too grumpy and that one too easily tossed off, there were a number of columns and articles which seemed, despite everything, to hold together. With a majority of the old columns and articles eliminated, what was left even made a book. This one.

What is this book, made up as it is of writing done over the years at odd intervals, finally about? It has been said by more than one writer that you write in order to find out what you think, and in going over several years' worth of writing I see a movement towards orthodox Christianity, coupled with a believe that orthodoxy has little to do with the certainties which some people demand of religion. This should not lead us to a secular resignation, or to the belief that because we cannot always be certain we must act without any clear conviction. Rather, we should see that the need to be right (which is so often a part of the quest for certainty) has very little to do with a love for the truth. It is rather a way of shoring up ego, even a way of protecting ourselves from the message of Christianity, which involves a transformation more thorough than we may like, at least at the level of consciousness to which we are most accustomed. True spirituality involves an awakening, a sharpening of awareness, and this goes against the grain of our culture, which seems to be built on distraction and violence. The forms of liturgy and spirituality which we need will in that sense be counter-cultural and involve a protest—a willingness to be unfashionable and to question the certainties of liberal and conservative Christianity alike.

These themes, anyway, seem to me to be the ones which are sounded in this book. I can see things here I disagree with now, years after having put them down on paper for the first time, and so I can hardly object to a reader's disagreement. Everything, though, was written in an effort at coming closer to clarity, and it will please me if, even through the process of disagreement, the reader finds the same thing happening.

— John Garvey

The Prematurely Saved

I've always believed in ecumenism. Some of my best friends are tolerant. But I may decide, before long, to give it up. At least I would like to begin asking some impolite questions which come to mind whenever I meet the prematurely saved, the "born-again"sorts who are given to lamenting their former existence (they drank, played cards, danced, thought about sex) and celebrating their present lives (now they do none of the above). If pressed—or even if they aren't—they will admit that Jews, Catholics, and even Protestants will go to hell unless they accept Jesus Christ as their personal savior.

My reason for feeling this way isn't simple resentment at being looked at as if I were a form of fuel. Not all of those people who talk about being saved bother me, as uncomfortable as I am with the language involved. On a long bus ride I once sat next to an old lady who said she was saved and worried about whether I was. After awhile I understood that she really *was* converted, she really had tried to give her life to God in a rare and important way. She was converted by her work with old and poor people, and by a minister who persuaded her that this should never be a matter of pride and self-righteousness.

The people I am worried about are the groups responsible to no one but TV audiences or other crowds, the people who are never involved in the self-critical discussion which true communities always share. They are everywhere, even into the technology of satellite television, a medium which, they insist, has been given them by God to get his word all over the planet. His word comes via stage sets equipped with rubber tree plants and hosts who yuck it up in between impassioned pleas to turn to the Lord. "Can a Christian really be depressed?" one of the joyboys asked recently. The answer was, of course, no. His wife, streaming tears and consequent mascara, testified some nights later that she really hadn't wanted to go on with this ministry but (guess what) Jesus gave her the courage. In the background there was a chorus of amens and praise Jesus; and though taste isn't everything, it is at least *something,* I thought, watching this version of the slow dissolve.

It isn't sincerity I wonder about here—if anything this sort of performance points up what a cheap virtue sincerity is—but the horror involved when you wrap up the gospel in the flag, sentimentality, individualism, and an uncritical view of American capitalism. Materialism is criticized, but this has less to do with the way we live than with the way we *feel* about how we live—and therein lies a clue.

The clue is that this is one more damned therapy, this wave of born-againism. It is functionally equivalent to *est* or TA or inner tennis. It makes you feel better about yourself and lets you be your own best friend and look after number one. This isn't necessarily anything more than silly, except for the fact that it is a growing phenomenon, with converts everywhere. One Quaker friend complained, "I hate the way they've co-opted the word 'Christian.' I hate it when they get some fink Catholic bishop or priest up there, to give the host an opportunity to trumpet the fact that even Catholics can be saved now."

The worst problem, though, is the idolatry. What gets blessed in all this? For any Christian a belief in perfectibility is a dangerous thing, and here we could get into a discussion of heresy as a meaningful social problem, but we won't. The more appropriate category might be whatever simple discipline it could take to frame the question, "What can it mean to say 'I am saved'?"

To say "I am saved" seems to say more about *me* than it does about God. If the universe is what I hope it is, God's will to save me, God's love for me, God's power to save everything created and God's love for what has been made—none of these things is in question. The problem is not with God's end of the equation but with my own. To say "I am saved"—as if it were my decision that made the big difference—seems arrogant, presumptuous. It isn't God I doubt, but myself. And to try to go beyond that—to arrive at a point where I trust myself enough to say "I am saved"—is less an act of faith in God than an act of faith in myself. That is precisely what the zeitgeist seems to want of me, but I'm not sure that it is God's will. The prematurely saved are asking us to arrive at conviction about this right now, as if it were our end of the deal, and not God's initiative, which mattered. When we locate and define the divine we create an idol. When we think we know God and try to use God for our ends, we are idolators. It is possible, I think, to have an idol and call it Jesus.

To be a follower of Jesus, do I have to know how I feel about it, or have a crystal clear sense of what it means to say that much of the creed? Or can I be led on, often in the dark, by the hope his words inspire, and the hope shown in his life, death, and resurrection? Does this need to involve a feeling of certainty or security? Or is there a danger in asking for these emotions? Too much recent evangelism has stressed the reassuring aspect of belief, as if it meant little or nothing that in the garden of Gethsemane "Jesus's soul was filled with dismay and dread." It is profoundly wrong, maybe even a surrender to evil, to expect to avoid dismay and dread. The vocation of a religion which is so intimately involved in the scandal of incarnation is a willingness to accept the agony of any flesh, including the darkness of unbelief and the knowledge of forsakenness. To say that I am sure of my salvation may be to try to hold on to something we are not allowed to keep, and to make of Jesus something merely comforting.

If religion is finally therapy, that makes sense. If it is not therapy, but clarity (which isn't necessarily so cozy a thing), then the people who have made Jesus the nicest talk-show host of them all will be in for a surprise which could awe them, delight them, or terrify them, but in any case will make them feel as foolish as we all ought to feel when we are too clear about what God wants of us.

The Temptation To Be Right

"Your eye is the light of your body; when your eye is sound, your whole body is full of light; but when it is not sound, your body is full of darkness." — Luke 11:34-35

The problem with Scripture is that we can think we know what it means, and feel that we've got it tied down: we know what we are supposed to do, how we are supposed to act, and the Book is there as a proof to back us up. Fundamentalists are good at this — it is practically their stock in trade — but Christians of every other stripe do the same thing. Pacifists point to Jesus telling Peter to put his sword away; militarists point to Luke 22, where Jesus tells his disciples that his original instructions to travel light, without provisions of any sort, have changed: "But now, let him who has a purse take it, and likewise a bag. And let him who has no sword sell his mantle and buy one." In *The Everlasting Gospel* Blake wrote, "The Vision of Christ that thou dost see/Is my Vision's Greatest Enemy. . . ./Thine loves the same world that mine hates,/Thy Heaven Doors are my Hell Gates."

We are tempted constantly to make use of Christ, or any vision of God. To the extent that we do this we make an idol of God. It is difficult for us to realize that it is possible for us to worship a false god, believing it with all our hearts to be true.

If we firmly believe that our cause is just, if it seems to us that anything which contradicts our vision is immoral, it is natural for us to seize upon the authority of the Bible or religious tradition to back us up. But in doing this we overlook the contradictory and equally authoritative passages of Scripture or elements of tradition; and we deal with this by saying that our own interpretation is a reflection of the *real* spirit of Scripture and the tradition of the church. Our opponents, who are apparently at a farther remove from the Holy Spirit than we are, don't understand this.

No matter how good our intentions are, or how noble the cause, this is a form of idolatry. What concerns us is not God's truth, which is at its depths unknowable and absolutely incomprehensible, but ideas which seem to us to be true. We can be so passionately attached to those ideas that we find it impossible to believe God doesn't share our opinion. This is not to say that our ideas may not in fact be noble and good and true. I am committed — or anyway I hope I am — to a nonviolent approach to life and morality. But I know I have been guilty of moving from this belief to an assertion that it is definitely and incontrovertibly to be found in Scripture and church tradition. And it can indeed be found there — along with a belief in the just-war theory and a theological defense of holy wars.

Is there any way out of this dilemma? It really *is* a dilemma, and one which matters deeply not only to our way of approaching morality at personal and social levels; it matters to our relationship with God. On the one hand, we cannot be so open-ended about moral and religious issues that absolutely anything is considered as true as anything else. On the other, we must avoid the idolatry which makes an idol of our own belief. The temptation is to look for some clear standard of truth — the ecumenical councils, the Bible, the papacy. But when we do this we see that some councils which were considered truly ecumenical at the time were later not accepted as such; we frequently find interpretations of the Bible in contradiction; we find that the papacy is as full of contradiction as any other source. So we look to the long haul, the beliefs that have survived and transcended all of this contradiction.

For Catholic and Orthodox Christians that includes a belief in creeds and sacraments, a general agreement with the councils of the early church, and a moral code which involves the commandments of the Old Testament and the spirit of the Beatitudes in the New Testament. There is little more than this. On many matters involving war and peace, sexual morality, politics, and the economy, we are given some help from the tradition. We also find some hindrances there too — defenses of slavery, for example — and as always there are contradictory directions. Trying to find a clear and unambiguous moral path by looking at Scripture and tradition is a little like trying to get clear and unambiguous directions while traveling in Ireland. It really can't be done, though everyone you talk to will be very sure.

We go at our relationship to God's truths in precisely the wrong way. We begin by assuming that they must correspond to and undergird our own. There are statements about prayer which contain a share of truth, but help to reinforce this dangerous tendency. They include the idea, frequently expressed, that our political and social involvements should be grounded in prayer. That is certainly true; the danger is that we will treat prayer as a form of therapy which exists to recharge our batteries so that we will have all the energy we need to do the really important work, which is not praying but activity of another sort. It is when this activity is most apparently virtuous that it is most likely to mislead us. We are not sufficiently humble before the fact that every convinced Nazi, fascist, Communist, crusader, Inquisitor, book-burner, vigilante, or member of a lynch mob is where he is because of the burning conviction that he is right, and stands where he stands against the forces of wrong-headedness or absolute evil. *Our* conviction, being right, is of course a different thing.

What we need is a truly radical humility, one which can abandon any need to be right. This is terribly difficult, because it could seem to be an indifference to truth. But our need to be right has nothing to do with any love of the truth at all — it is essential for us to understand this. The strangeness of Christ is a lesson for us: the contradictions are calls to a wider and more difficult view of life than we want. After his Resurrection he appeared not as he might have been expected to appear, but as a stranger. We are told, "Be careful lest the light in you be darkness." He does not say that it will not appear to us to be light; he cautions us that what seems to us to be light may in fact not be.

In his essay "The Unity of the Triune God" (printed in *St. Vladimir's Theological Quarterly,* Number 3, 1984) Jurgen Moltmann quotes St. Gregory of Nyssa: "Concepts create idols; only wonder comprehends anything." People kill one another over idols. Wonder makes us fall to our knees. Revelation tells us that we are created from nothing, called into being and given a freedom which is not at all easy to comprehend, and can never be comprehended completely. Prayer is the way towards seeing what all of this means, because in prayer — in the effort to be attentive — we learn how radically contingent we are, how absolutely dependent on someone unknowable. That we have been called forth from nothingness, in love, is revealed, not as a fact but as an openness which can be responded to honestly only with an emptiness of our own, an acknowledgment of our absolute insufficiency. This emptiness is the place where compassion can be born, because it is absolutely shared with everything else in creation it is the common ground of our being.

"When the eye is sound, the whole body is full of light." How can we be sure that the eye is sound? It could be that sureness is not what is called for here, but humility. Jesus tells us not to look for ways to be sure, but rather to take care. Gregory of Nyssa's words suggest that a lack of wonder leads to idolatry. Only a lack of wonder could lead us to look at what Scripture and tradition tell us, and come up with concepts. This is not only the recurrent temptation of theologians, but of any churchgoer who believes that what Christianity involves is clear and simple, a matter of having the right politics or ethics. Political or ethical thinking which is unredeemed by compassion leads us to think of ourselves as sufficient, because we are right. Our rightness fills us up. It leads us to ignore the emptiness that is part of being created. So much of what we regard as evil is a result of trying to fill up that emptiness false-ly. Bertolt Brecht's poem, "Concerning the Infanticide, Maria Farrar" (from *Selected Poems,* translated and edited by H.R. Hays, Grove, 1959) is right to the point. It is an excruciating description of agony, and ends,

She brings home to you all men's sin.
You who bear pleasantly between clean sheets
And give the name 'blessed' to your womb's weight
Must not damn the weakness of the outcast,
For her sin was black but her pain was great.
Therefore, I beg you, check your wrath and scorn
For man needs help from every creature born.

Quivers of Conscience

In one of Peter DeVries's wonderful novels a man is forced to listen to a writer he cannot abide read a tear-jerking story which is as manipulative as it could be, and yet (as Galileo is said to have said under his breath) it moves! I wish I could offer a citation, chapter and verse, but as I recall it DeVries says of his unwilling listener, "His sneer was strangled on a sob." The DeVries line sums up an aspect of our character which takes up lots of space. There ought to be a word for it. It would not be as simple as hypocrisy, because hypocrisy has come to suggest a degree of conscious self-deception. Self-deception itself is not good enough; too broad. To get at it we need — pay attention now — examples.

It is a common and embarrassing experience to find ourselves moved against our wills. The sentimental movie, the late-night rerun showing a kid with a quivering lip and dead parents, cops with rescued puppies, name it; we love it, in some part of the soul. A few years ago Americans loved pictures of wide-eyed and rather solemn-looking children, the kitschiest of them all showed John-John Kennedy saluting his father's coffin. Apparently a similar sort of sentimental art is popular in Iran, where pictures of young weeping women are popular.

Far be it from me to complain about being an easy touch for these things; I'm the sort of person who can cry every time Old Yaller dies. But I wonder what it means. I know from personal experience that it has nothing to do with being a decent human being. I think all it proves is that I am not dead yet. A pin could do the same thing, but wouldn't return the ego-satisfying dividends. We would like to think that being moved this way proves that we are compassionate people; if we can be moved to tears by something certifiably sad, we must have a heart after all.

To interpret this quiver of consciousness — a little like the experiments Galvani did when he ran electricity into severed frog legs and made them jerk — as a sign of decency is obscene. It is said that Hitler cried at the death of his canary. I think we tend to use this reaction to keep ourselves from becoming aware of how truly stony-hearted we are. It is certainly less costly to be moved to tears than to be moved to action. Our teariness at the appropriate moments is a matter of convention, an observance of a piety upon which everyone agrees. It is an emotional token, advanced across the board to show that we are basically decent and sensitive people.

During the Christmas season these tokens are waved all over the place. Newspapers run campaigns to raise money for the "neediest" (there is something Victorian about the sound of that word), and assistance finds its way to people who are apparently invisible the rest of the year. In my home town the local paper (generally right-wing and more or less quiet about what goes on in the state capital, which wouldn't be so bad if the state capital didn't happen to be here) calls its annual "be nice" campaign "Friend-in-Need." Fletcher Farrar, Jr., editor of the alternative weekly *Illinois Times,* has made the important point that the local daily's editorial page ordinarily does everything it can to discourage any governmentally-sponsored measure which might help the poor.

It's a little like the old joke, "A friend in need is a pest"... except at Christmas, when he gives us an opportunity to act like Scrooge running out for a goose. We put from our minds the fact that we will probably try to find a way to tax the goose-bones the day after the end of the holiday season. At times like this, or at any of the other times when we are moved to what we think of as compassion, we take our sensitivity as something which all by itself validates us as moral people. The homeless and hungry and handicapped go back to being nameless spongers once more, when the Christmas season is over. No matter — the tears we shed then show that we really do care, we aren't bad folk after all, we can think well of ourselves.

This moral tokenism isn't confined to our seasonal self-contradictions. People live by such tokens all year round, form friendships around them, look for the latest variations on the theme, "what belief makes me decent?" It is like a form of war-paint at parties where people don't know one another very well: above their heads, in comic-strip balloons, you can read "Mahler; Updike; Gary Hart; too-bad-about-starving-Ethiopians; I miss the style of the forties." He's talking to "I still get mad about Watergate; what they are doing in Afghanistan is awful; Howard Hawkes and Hitchcock are my favorite directors; I would never buy war-toys for my children." You can tell fairly quickly whom you will be able to talk with next time without having your own tokens shoved aside too rudely; you can find out whom to approach for help during the next political campaign, and whom to avoid. That shorthand may be useful in its way, but we talk and think this way for another and less obvious reason. Having the right opinion somehow makes us good. We take our own opinions as proof of our moral righteousness.

There seems to be a human need to identify the self — or whatever it is that we come to identify as the self — with something larger. The self is itself frequently no more than a bag of disparate reactions. But outrage over the "right" things or the "wrong" things makes us real; so does political or moral or religious passion applied in any direction. This process of identifying ourselves with the right passion is made easy with simplification — better the bumper sticker or button or subscription to the right magazine than the more difficult work of thought and (God forbid) any self-doubt about the issue or range of issues at hand. There are appeals made to us, through carefully bought mailing lists, which pose us against all the others — "the others" being those people who are bigoted, racist, unenlightened, narrow. Unlike us, in other words. This ought to disturb us. Instead, it makes us feel good. We enjoy the distance, the little lift we get when we see the neighbor's bumper sticker and thank God we didn't vote that way.

Our sick status is this: we love all the tokens which make us different from our neighbor. Or rather, not from our neighbor but from the wrong sort of neighbor — the one whose opinion or set of opinions shows him to have the wrong war paint, the unacceptable perspective. I have had a lot of advertisements mailed to me, for magazines and political causes, which had as their main appeal the notion that by responding I could prove myself different. The difference had to do with sophistication and political enlightenment. But what sort of enlightenment is it that depends on maintaining a distance between oneself and the other, the fool out there? By responding to that appeal to my worst sympathies, don't I come close to answering — in a way which ought to terrify me — the question, "Who is my neighbor?"

Christianity and Power

Jesus said a number of things about power and power-lessness. In Luke's account of the temptation of Jesus, Satan tells Jesus that power over all of the kingdoms of the world has been given into his hands, and Jesus refused to pay Satan homage in order to receive power. When James and John show a desire for power in the kingdom they believe Jesus will establish, he tells them "You know that in the world, rulers lord it over their subjects, and their great men make them feel the weight of authority; but it shall not be so with you. Among you, whoever wants to be great must be your servant, and whoever would be first must be the willing slave of all—like the Son of Man; he did not come to be served, but to serve, and to surrender his life as a ransom for many."

The theme of becoming great by becoming least recurs throughout the Gospels, and it is connected with compassion and forgiveness. "Whatever you do to the least of these, you do to me . . . Love your enemies, do good to those who hate you, pray for those who persecute you . . . You will not be forgiven unless you forgive your brother from the bottom of your heart."

These statements of Jesus move us; they convince us that he was a special sort of person, uniquely compassionate. We regard these words with reverence, as we should; we would resent it if someone were to scorn them. But we do not take them straight, as instructions aimed at us. Or we accept them as a kind of unkept promise: someday we will know what it means to love our enemies, to serve rather than to be served, to forgive from the bottom of our hearts. At present we regard these counsels as incapable of fulfillment, as if Jesus were less than realistic.

Can families, businesses, or governments be run on Christian principles? For example, can a society regard a Charles Manson as one of the least of the brethren? Can a society regard someone outside the borders of the state which claims to represent society as a brother or sister, someone I must die for if necessary, but never kill? And if the state finds it necessary to kill either the criminal within or the enemy without, isn't that command of the state and its acceptance by Christians a confession that Jesus's words are not adequate to all situations, that they are limited in application, smaller than the fullness of human being?

One response to the words of Christ involves an interior change. We are told that we must not bear the napalmed child any malice, or enjoy the spectacle of the dying criminal, or delight in the killing of the enemy conscript. This approach allows us to feel Christian, while assuring the inefficacy of Jesus's teaching at any level other than an emotional or esthetic one. If, however, Jesus's words demand a change which will not allow us to kill the criminal or the enemy, the basis of much of our political life is shaken.

The question of Christianity's relationship to power was clearly a problem from the beginning. Although it would be an oversimplification to say that the early church was pacifist, it would be a much greater oversimplification to deny it. Christian allegiance to the state was heavily qualified, and killing, whether in war or for reasons of state, was discouraged where it was not grounds for excommunication.

The relationship of Christianity to power is more complicated than one would think, looking at much of the current comment on the relations between church and state in places as different as Poland, the United States, El Salvador, and the Philippines. Most commentators assume that the church is doing a good thing (if the church supports the sort of power the commentator likes), a bad thing (if it does not), or a forbidden thing (if the commentator is the sort who thinks that religion must never have any effect at all other than an emotional one, on those who happen to be attending a religious service).

What is not often considered in this context is the fact that Christianity is about the thorough transformation of the human being, a transformation which happens at the collective level as well as the individual level. This transformation is brought about by God, not by any institution. It is made possible by an openness to the work of God in us, an openness which trusts that God's working is a real thing, not a metaphor for the ethics of the believer but the source of that ethics, a source which the believer must always realize that he does not himself possess and cannot manipulate.

Christianity is not unique in having accepted the patronage and protection of the rich and powerful. But because the words of Christ challenge conventional views of authority the problem is particularly pointed in Christian history. Many of the indictments that have been brought against the church have involved the manifestations of Christianity as a kind of power. The list is ugly and familiar: we have all heard of the Crusades and the Inquisition, the persecution of Jews, the genocidal crusade of Cromwell in Ireland, countless conversions at swordpoint, the forced conversion of Orthodox to Catholicism under the treaty of Brest-Litovsk, and the more recent forced conversion of Eastern-rite Catholics to Orthodoxy under Soviet sponsorship—no one, Catholic, Protestant, or Orthodox, mainstream churchman or Anabaptist, gets off untainted. And the problem is an ancient one: the first ecumenical council (if you except the council of Jerusalem) was convened not by a pope or by bishops, but by the authority of the emperor, whose influence was, if not decisive, nevertheless felt. Important doctrinal formulations involved not only Christian dogma but also national and regional allegiances, imperial and anti-imperial politics.

Christians have accepted, with varying degrees of ease, forms of authority which are, in practice, everything Jesus said his followers were not to be. If we believe that it is the might of the state which protects us, if we believe that we must rely on force, our claim to trust God is to at least a certain extent a sentimentality. This is not our only form of idolatry; the need for financial security is another. And no one is completely free of idolatry; even voluntary poverty and nonviolence can become idols, particularly when we believe that we possess them as virtues. But our willingness to accept power and the allegiances which demand the use of force against other human beings has been the source of more misery in our time than anything else. Faced with it we feel a certin helplessness, as if there were simply no alternative to choosing one violent side over another. There is nothing hypocritical about the claims many of us make to be Christian while at the same time we feel the need to accept violence as a tragic necessity; this is a genuine difficulty for many people, we experience it as an agony which has no alternative. But how limited is this point of view?

I read recently of an Aztec sacrifice, made to appeal to the rain God. A child would be selected and taken to the edge of a river and beaten until it began to weep. The adults, moved by the child's suffering, wept too, and their weeping would turn to mourning as the child was drowned by someone sacred; this was a necessary horror, a sacrifice involving real tears and real tragedy. The tears were all genuine, no doubt, and the ones which were not probably felt to those who forced themselves to shed tears the way our own false tears do: we know we should feel what we do not feel.

We are horrified by the thought of deliberate human sacrifice, the picture of the heart torn out and still bleeding in the hand of the Aztec priest. It horrifies us in a way which Hiroshima does not. Our horror may be greater where limited ritual death is concerned because, unlike the death of hundreds of thousands of people killed for strategic reasons, death on an altar suggests a demand by God for blood. A divine demand for blood horrifies us. A governmental demand for blood, on the other hand, does not. I have a strong feeling that a sensitive Aztec observer felt keenly both the necessity of ritual murder, and the profound sadness which accompanies the knowledge that the world simply couldn't exist in any other way. The Aztecs might have felt that they were participants in a nightmare from which there was no awakening. We believe that the nightmarish quality of their ritual consists in believing it to have been necessary. We will have made some progress when our own situation appears as nightmarish to us, and our own vision as narrow and unnecessarily murderous as theirs was.

Some Difficulties of Modern Spirituality

"Spirituality" should be removed as a category, a kind of subset, part of the business of being Christian. We may have to speak of it this way once in a while in order to get our bearings, but to consider spirituality a part of being Christian is a bit like speaking of being conscious as part of being alive. Spirituality is essential to Christianity; it has to do not only with the formal aspects of trying to pray, but with the moment-to-moment consciousness of the Christian, because our goal is finally to learn what Paul meant when he asked his readers to "pray without ceasing." I would also like to point out that it is not a good idea to ask at the start what spirituality can "do for you," and to suggest something which makes me as uncomfortable as it may make you: I think prayer and fasting go together, and that both lead to a simplification of life, even to voluntary poverty.

The purpose of spirituality does not vary from life to life. It is rather the response each of us must try to make to the question, "Who can look upon the face of the Lord and live?" Not me, not as I am now. Not you, I'd bet. Spirituality is our cooperation in the process God initiated when he called us to be Christians, the process by which we become — in the words of the Fathers — "gods by adoption."

It is assumed by a lot of people that it is more difficult to be Christian now than it was in earlier times, when Christianity was supported by social, political, and cultural props on all sides. This belief would seem to be given some weight in view of the great numbers of people who find it quite easy to leave traditional religious backgrounds for more secular values, apparently feeling no loss in the process. While it is true that this climate does create unique difficulties — difficulties which are not at all unlike the ones which the first Christians faced — it does not make being a Christian any more difficult than it ever was. What is gone is the common consolation of believing that Christianity can be equated with acceptable morality and good citizenship, combined with church-going. It is more obviously a *task* to be Christian now, a vocation, and some of the obstacles to its fulfillment are unique to our time and our culture.

Before going on, I must make some of my own assumptions clear; what follows hinges on them. First of all, I believe that in the field of spirituality no breakthroughs will be made. Unlike scriptural studies, for example, there is nothing new to be discovered here. The only cumulative effect of lived spirituality happens in the soul of the person who prays, and I believe we have the testimony of men and women who went as far as they could go. We may learn from other traditions, and there will be new masters of the spiritual life, but what we are offered will not get us beyond *The Philokalia* or *The Cloud of Unknowing*. Another of my assumptions is that the orthodox approach to prayer is the best — that is, the insistence that it demands time, some solitude, regularity, and self-discipline. This means that it is best to set aside some time every day to sit quietly for awhile and do nothing but pray, or try to pray.

Any sort of living which does not allow enough time for solitude and prayer should be seen as a genuine problem for Christians. Most of us have more time than we think, but if anything characterizes our time it is the hunger for distraction and the unwillingness to face being alone, in silence. (There was a time when the rhythms of work, or the necessity of getting from one place to another on foot or on horseback, forced people to take time.) We are made nervous by anything which could lead us to confront our inner emptiness, and just sitting makes us more nervous than anything else. But our desire for distraction is deadly. Until we confront the swarming confusion which *is* our ordinary consciousness, the lens through which we filter the world, we do not know who we are, or how empty we are. This experience rises to confront the person who prays or meditates, at one time or another, and it reveals the desire for distraction as one of the many desires which, in the chilling words of one Orthodox author, lead us around "like captive corpses."

I realize that there is on the part of some writers a reluctance to recommend regular periods of prayer; the fear is that these will be seen as ends in themselves, and an idol will be made of mere routine. There is a similar prejudice against the use of such techniques as the use of a repeated prayer (like the "Jesus prayer" practiced by Orthodox Christians and the Catholic rosary) or disciplined meditation. The argument is that we should be more spontaneous, less tied down. We should use our own words, not words composed by someone else. There is truth in both objections — a period of prayer can become too routine, and the technique which can lead us to heartfelt prayer can be confused with prayer itself. And certainly it is a good thing to pray in one's own words. But the argument in favor of regular periods of prayer, a set time limit, and so forth, seems to me much stronger.

First of all, prayer which is not regular is likely to depend on how we feel. If we don't feel like praying, we are likely not to — unless we have determined that (for example) every afternoon we will set aside half an hour or so, no matter how we feel. The point here is that prayer is not an option for Christians. It is essential. The discipline of regular prayer, like the discipline of a repeated prayer, can teach us the most basic lesson: how wandering and frivolous our ordinary concerns are, how ungathered and rootless our consciousness usually is. Trying again and again to return to the essential point of prayer may be frustrating, but it is the beginning of prayer; and the alternative is not really prayer, but a form of self-expression which frequently uses the word "God."

This may sound severe, but there is a kind of religiosity which is itself a danger to genuine spirituality. That is the sort of prayer which is recommended almost as therapy, the belief that we should pray because it will do such great things for us, make us feel better, give us self-confidence, and so forth. I honestly believe that this use of the name of God is idolatry.

We do not know who we are. We have been shown what we might be in Jesus Christ. We do not know much about how we should act, or what we should want, or what it would be like to be truly Christian. In prayer we must stand before God as we are, confused and empty, full of a nearly uncontrolled potential for the deepest evil and the heights of sanctity. We must do this as we are, not as we would like to be. We do not pray to reinforce a "positive self-image," or for that matter a negative one. We should have no self-image at all, or at least confess that every idea of self we have is idolatrous.

We do not know God. We know of God only through scripture, the lives of those who have known him best, and even perhaps some events in our own past — but this knowledge of God does not let us grasp him, and the One we stand before is unknowable. In prayer we bring our own darkness, need, and emptiness, and stand before a deeper silence, trusting in the promise of God that we will be transformed into what he wants us to be. Our attempts to impose our own agenda on God, or decide in advance how we should feel about prayer, or what prayer will do for us, get in God's way.

Although the personality of Jesus is hidden from us, one of the things we do know about him is that he felt the need to pray, and required solitude for prayer. There are people who say that the right sort of action *is* prayer, but this is only partially true. Action can be prayerful, but its prayerful quality procedes from the direct prayer which happens in solitude. Without time devoted exclusively to prayer the danger is that God will become an idea, and the presence of God will become a feeling we look for.

Another thing Jesus felt the need to do was fast. There is a danger in thinking that this was done simply for our example. Jesus was not, of course, someone who acted human; he was everything a human being is, and he did the things human beings need to do in order to be children of God.

But fasting requires some explanation. It is nothing like a deal with God ("I'll fast if you do me a favor") or a desperate

29

attempt to get God's attention ("See how serious I am"), but a way of confronting ourselves at levels which may otherwise never be touched. The defense of fasting is, of course, not merely rational or psychological. It is so well grounded in tradition that it shouldn't require defending; Jesus fasted and recommended it, so did Paul, so did the Fathers of the Church, and the fasts of the Orthodox church are strict ones. But tradition itself is in disrepute, and an additional reason may be in order — a reason which might lead us to view traditional wisdom, which knew it all along, with more sympathy.

It is easy enough to say that Christianity involves a willingness to obey God, to move with God's will, leaving everything else behind. But to say this from *our* perspective, unchallenged by anything other than a theoretical alternative, leaves us in illusion — as if we were not at this moment called to be aware of God's will, and immediately available for God's service. The illusion is reinforced by the fact that most of us are living in comfort — which is to say, we eat and drink more or less as we like, we arrange our hours (beyond the necessity our work forces us into) to suit ourselves, or our families; and when we move out of ourselves enough to accommodate wife, husband, or child, we think of this as virtue.

Fasting goes against the grain. To refrain from meat, dairy products, alcohol, or fish (this range of foods is chosen only because it is a traditional one) can make us edgy. We are made aware of how our desires really determine us and rule our days. To refrain from eating or drinking for awhile, and to see, as a result, how dominant our will can be, is to face an aspect of ourselves that only fasting can teach us. At the very least, fasting disabuses us of the notion that we are generous by nature. It also forces our attention to prayer (perhaps because there is no other reason to put up with the discomfort, a reminder which has something in common with the old joke about the man who beat the mule over its head with a two-by-four, not to be cruel but just to get his attention); and hunger does produce a clarity of attention which isn't there after a good meal. Another embarrassing fact is that one of our fasts would look, to many people barely alive now, like a feast.

Fasting is a matter of attention, focus, and clarity. It is a way of "glorifying God in your bodies," according to Paul's recommendation. At the very least it is a reminder that our ordinary over-consumption should not be considered a norm.

It also has social implications. If fasting can teach us what we do not need, it can teach us what we can afford to give away. The opinion of the early Church about property was unanimous: if you have more than you need, you owe it to the person who needs it. There is a form of conservative Christianity which reduces this sort of idea to "the social gospel" and claims that it is a turning away from a more spiritual Christianity. The social gospel needs no more defense than Matthew 25, where Jesus says that what we do not do for the least human being, we refuse to do for God. Since I also fail to live up to the expectation so clearly spelled out, I would like a softer interpretation, but I don't think one can be found. Jesus' words here are not at all ambiguous. I may be in trouble for failing to take them to heart at the depth I must, but it would be even worse to pretend that they meant something else — something like "It's all right to live the way you do, as long as you don't get too attached to it." The mysterious words about "the sin against the Holy Spirit which will not be forgiven" might apply to the attempt to make Jesus an advocate on behalf of my way of life. In a world in which people are hungry it seems obscene to me to defend having more than you need, and it is especially ugly to use the gospel in the argument. I am not at all concerned here with what governments ought to do about poverty, as important a question as that is. It does seem important, whatever governments do, for Christians to live in a way which exhibits the concern of God for humanity. In a hungry world, this cannot be exhibited by people who have more than they need.

And almost all of us do. This is a major personal problem, for each Christian, and a problem for the Church as a whole. The immediate temptation is to look at the enormity of the problem and give up. But there are some prophetic voices here, and even a prophetic silence. The community of Taizé (the ecumenical French monastic community) has suggested that

Christians move slowly but deliberately to a more austere way of life. In a "letter to the People of God" the Taizé community has suggested that people young enough to do so should divest themselves of unnecessary wealth, searching for ways to share what they have; and they make the sensible recommendation that this be done with slow deliberation, over a period of years, but with simplification as the goal. The Little Brothers of Jesus have for years shared the lives of the poor, in the poorest sections of the world's cities, while spending time each day in prayer. Their special vocation is a silent one: they do not proselytize, and although sometimes they have been regarded as threatening by governments used to a more compliant and predictable form of Christianity, their concern is not essentially political.

How can families do this? I realize that there is a way of thinking which exempts families from such concerns; that isn't our "vocation." It would be a lot easier to agree than to disagree with this, but in conscience I can't. When "family" becomes the excuse for failing to respond to the gospel it is one more idol. But it is also clear that a response to the gospel which is inconsiderate (in all the meanings that word has) is not really a response to the gospel at all. Obviously, a family should not be swept from one way of life into another on a wave generated by the enthusiasm of one or two of its members. The specific way in which a family will make the journey from the way of life our society recommends, to the way the gospel indicates, is something which will depend upon the ages of children, the willingness of husband or wife, and so forth — but the fact that the work is complicated doesn't absolve us from trying, as well as we can manage, to do it. One help can be a close association with an existing communal group. There are a few groups of families who do try to have all things in common and share a life of prayer. There are monasteries and convents, and there is the continuing radical witness of the Catholic Worker movement. Being close to any of the people, or groups of people, who are trying to take the gospel to heart can help, and show some specific ways.

Granted, this seems a very fluid sort of recommendation.

But that may have something to do with the time we're in. Monasticism was at first a lay movement (and the attempts to absorb it into the structures of the official church led Cassian to say that monks should avoid bishops and women, since neither would give them any peace). It could be that our time will see the working out of a familial equivalent of the radical witness monks once gave.

I can see at the end of this that my assumption is the corruption of our society, the belief that there isn't much in it which can be redeemed. That *is* my view, and it is difficult for me to understand how anyone can look at our century and feel very hopeful about anything other than deliberate attempts to challenge the assumptions which have brought the world through death camps, Hiroshima, Vietnam, Cambodia, the Gulag, Biafra, and an easy acceptance of torture, the death penalty, and abortion. Our society is built on greed, waste, and the creation of false needs. The alternative to it is soul-killing and totalitarian. A friend of mine once suggested that the basic moral problem is, "How will I raise my children?" Now more than ever the answer is, "In fear and trembling."

Of course, getting through life has always involved fear and trembling, and in this respect our terrible time has a place with every other era. In any era the question "Will the Son of Man find faith when he comes?" must be answered very personally; he'll find me, most probably, trying to make excuses.

Truth Or Consequences

Toward the beginning of the Iranian hostage crisis I was talking to a man who believed strongly that immediate punitive action was necessary: unless we made Iran hurt—and this hurting had to be obvious—we would be sitting ducks in a world full of reasonable grudges against America. If the lives of the hostages were lost in the process, too bad; their lives are less important than an international realization that America can't be taken on so cheaply. This realization would preserve more lives in the long run than would be lost because of our show of strength.

The political columnist George Will has defended this line of thinking as well as it can be defended. It appalls me in just about every way; but it haunts me too, since most liberal and left-wing answers to it are deficient. The same deficiency shows up in a number of other places, for instance in the way we talk about Vietnam, or capital punishment, or abortion. This came home to me during a hearing of the Illinois house, which was debating the reinstitution of capital punishment. A lawyer from the American Civil Liberties Union (we will call him Mr. Wimp) was being interrogated by a thick-necked, red-faced legislator from a Chicago suburb, who described a particularly brutal rape and then leaned forward to ask, "Mr. Wimp, do you mean to tell me that this animal should be allowed to live, and we should pay his room and board for the rest of his life?" He exaggerated his incredulity, of course, because he knows that this is exactly what Wimp meant to tell him, pointing out along the way that capital punishment was not a deterrent, or at least that its deterrent value had not been proven; that capital punishment was inflicted disproportionately on poor people and members of racial minorities; that it might even cause crime, since if you know that for one murder you will be fried, why not commit another. All sound reasons. Then another legislator, not at all a John Wayne sort, asked Mr. Wimp a very good question: if the deterrent value of capital punishment were proven, and if it were more evenly distributed across class and color lines, would he then support it? The answer wasn't an answer—just a stammer of sorts, a repetition of belief that there was no such evidence and no real way of gathering it—and as I listened I realized that what had happened was typical of a lot of liberal thought. Any time we are in danger of committing a moral absolute we scramble wildly in every other direction—let's see, where's the evidence, hand me those statistics—because it seems so damned unenlightened and even stuffy to say "I am against capital punishment because a decent society does not kill people, even if it works." This declaration leads to the sensible question, why not, to which there is finally one answer: because human life is holy.

Mr. Wimp probably hates words like "holy," but knows in some gloomy recess of his soul (he probably hates words like soul, too) that even if capital punishment were a proven deterrent, he would still oppose it, but he isn't sure why. Since there can be no absolutes—this is an article of his faith—he must find sensible reasons, reasons which can be backed up with evidence, for his belief that capital punishment is wrong, that we should not have done what we did in Vietnam, that we should not drop bombs on Iran.

But what if the evidence goes the other way? That's inconceivable; it isn't allowed to point in any uncomfortable direction. But that rubs us up against an absolute again.

People who believe power can be used compassionately often make assumption which is a hybrid of Christian puritanism and the rationalism of the enlightenment. The assumption, loosely stated, is that what is right will be socially valuable. It will have a practical application which will work out to the political advantage of everyone. The negative side of this assumption is that what we know to be bad (violence, coercion, threats, deception) will not work well in the practical realm. Virtue will succeed, vice will fail.

What if our opponents are right? What if capital punishment does deter crime, abortion does relieve some burdens, and strong military action does prevent the rise of certain forms of tyranny? I am not arguing that practical arguments for doing what is right should be discarded. What I am suggesting is this: it may be that there are instances where doing what is right means that you will not succeed; you will lose, and suffer for it. Our streets may be less safe because our system of justice tries to be fair. Our country may be weaker, and is certainly perceived as a weaker country, because of our defeat in Vietnam. And if we do not try to build up our weapons systems, we may in fact wind up weaker than our enemies. We seem to want it both ways—to be as strong and respected as Rome, but not pagan; to be safe, and free; to be good, and powerful.

Our ideas of good and evil are the legacies of people who believed in absolutes. Our society is not allowed to admit them. Insofar as this prevents us from living under a theocracy or any unquestionable orthodoxy, it is a good thing. But it leaves a hole which needs filling. The ancient Greeks, Jews, and Christians were able to consider the possibility that virtue might mean dying, and that there might be instances under which survival and safety could only be had through treacherous means. We can't discuss such issues as nuclear disarmament, capital punishment, abortion, the use of force or the obligations of rich nations to poor ones, in any significant way if our strongest argument is that the right course of action is necessarily the most practical one. What if it isn't, our opponents ask? In a society with no feeling for absolutes we are tongue-tied. It can even come to this: in a situation where we can play one of two roles, victim and victimizer, the right thing is to be the victim. This was the triumph of the mother of the seven brothers whose story is told in Maccabees; it is the cross. In the only reading our culture allows, it doesn't get you anywhere.

Sick, Sick, Sick — Or Evil

"Modern Science has painted a picture of the universe which is humbling to the human ego. But while destroying astronomical geocentrism, it has assumed what might be called a psychological geocentrism. What are the limitations of knowledge that man's ordinary state of consciousness places upon him? This seems never to be a question for the modern temper." — Jacob Needleman, in *The New Religions* (Doubleday, 1970).

First there was Jonestown, the pathetic story of people who called Jim Jones "daddy," and then a couple of weeks later police in a Chicago suburb were digging up bodies under the home of a man who dressed up as a clown to entertain children. We are repelled, fascinated and numbed as we read about events like these. Our usual response is to say that such people must be sick. They *must* be—right?

I wonder about that. I wonder about our inability to use the word "evil." Perhaps it is the fact mentioned recently by a friend of mine, a psychologist: we have psychologized all our experience, as if a description were the same thing as an explanation. Having found a few clear patterns we think we have all the answer we need. Adultery, for example, isn't evil anymore; it is hardly a choice. It is a way of telling your mate something, telling yourself something, a response to deprivation, whatever—but it isn't wrong. We know better now. There are people who, over the last several years, claimed to be experts in something called "values clarification". It's role is to help us "find out what our values are," as if values lay deep in our psyches, to be uncovered like buried treasure. When in our ordinary experience moral choice is so reduced, we are really at a loss when we bump into something spectacularly hideous.

The word "sick" is being stretched very thin these days. Manson, Hitler, Idi Amin, mass murderers, cooperators in mass murder, Calley, the Shah's torturers—all are either "products of the system" (so choice isn't involved), or they are "sick," part of a class which includes people who get migraines, flu, colds and measles. Ah, but this is mental illness, a very mysterious thing. . . .

I want to suggest this heresy: Jim Jones, Charles Manson, and all their company are creatures like us. We could do what they did; we would even be likely to, under conditions which brought us to the moments at which they made their worst choices. To say that they are "sick" allows us to avoid this possibility. It makes them *other.* They caught some special virus, some weird bug that makes them *not like us*—and that's what counts. If they were brought to the dreadful places in which they made their fame by anything involving choice, we're all in trouble.

I remember an interview with a refugee from Uganda, a man who had been prominent in the government there. American newsmen asked if he thought Idi Amin was insane. No, he answered, he isn't. He knows precisely what he is doing. He is evil. The newsmen persisted: of course he must be sick...how else could he do those things? The Ugandan answered that as long as the newsmen thought Amin was sick, they couldn't understand what was going on in Uganda. And of course they couldn't. It is less unsettling to think that a man like Idi Amin is ill than to think that he might have chosen to be what he is.

But given Charles Manson's sad foster home rambling, Jim Jones's lonely childhood, and later his being the object (or victim) of an adulation which could turn almost anyone so alone from the start into a false messiah—given things like this, who can speak simply of evil?

The point is not to speak of it simply, only to speak of it at all. In the twentieth century (the time of Auschwitz, the Gulag, China's rape of Tibet, Hiroshima) we find it difficult to accept the fact that there is something which does not love humanity, but delights in negation and destruction. It is not at all obvious in most of its workings; it can enter our lives through our need to be loved, our desire to be regarded as important and interesting, our fear of inner emptiness. It is there at the center of what we want, or think we want. As disturbing as it may be to think that there is a real connection between our own casual insensitivity and the crime of the most vicious murderer, if thousands of years of testimony about the human heart have anything to tell us, there is a link. The power of evil can work its way up from the heart's emptiness to murder. Hubert Selby's novel *The Demon* is a compelling fictional portrait of a real process: a sexual obsession which seems light and innocent enough at the start leads, finally, to murder and suicide.

The first time you encounter the writing of a saint who claims to be the most evil of men, you are likely to think of this as a sort of bragging. How could he be, really? Murderers must be worse, of course; what is an unkind flare-up,immediately regretted,next to murder? The point, of course, is that the person whose life is lived at the edge of religious awareness is conscious, moment to moment, of choices which are only apparent to the rest of us (and to the murderer, for that matter) once in awhile. When Saint Anthony went into the desert to face himself and God, he did not find in himself a poor self-image. He found demons. (The most impressive Christian I have met said to me once, "If God can save me, he can save anyone." There was no false piety, there was nothing at all false, in his words.)

There is no denying that an extreme consciousness of the choice between good and evil can be taken too far. A sense of life which is too constantly critical can lead to neurotic misery. But the belief that as we are, we are more or less all right — this is crazy. It means that we are willing to settle for being less than we *must* be; every great religious tradition is clear about that much. The religious tradition most readers of this magazine are familiar with speaks not only of a good God, but also of the "prince of this world," the world's tormentor. There is a bad, if classical, idea that evil is merely an absence of good, a lack. But it is not a lack which had the power to murder millions under Hitler; it was an acquiescence to evil, which is real. It is not enough to look at the economic conditions of post-World War I Germany to explain the holocaust, nor can the bloodshed in Uganda be explained by searching for clues in Idi Amin's childhood. At what point does choice enter these things? It may not be possible to pin that one down scientifically, but it is an absolutely essential question. Maybe because it defies our current demand for objectivity, for the appearance of hard scientific data (a superstition as silly as any), the question of choice will continue to be ignored. Never mind the fact that answering it is quite literally a matter of life and death.

Choice As Absolute

This is not about abortion. I have to make that clear because it begins with some language which showed up in an ad sponsored by the Religious Coalition for Abortion Rights, an ad with which I disagree, but my disagreement with the ad and its sponsors isn't the main point here. What I am interested in is the way the assumptions we make about what it means to be human can show up where we don't expect to meet them, like plants which thrust through the pavement or grow in gutters at the tops of buildings. Rhetoric is meant to convince, to seem inarguably right; it grabs you by the lapels. In this debate and in many others one form of rhetoric meets another. The anti-abortion people call themselves pro-life, and who can oppose them? No one wants to be anti-life. Their opponents call themselves pro-choice—and who wants to be anti-choice? But the structure of an argument can't help revealing the assumptions of its maker, and the language in this ad reveals assumptions which are fascinating.

What caught my eye was a couple of sentences—or rather, a sentence and sentence fragment, since the ad is written in a style I first noticed in old Volkswagen ads, where a sentence is followed by brief non-sentences, something like this: "You'll like it. Because it's built right. The way you want it." The emphysemic style doesn't make the thought behind the sentence and its trailing fragments necessarily wrong, but in this case the device underscored precisely the arguable assumption. This is what the ad said: "We believe abortion is an individual decision. And therefore your God-given right."

Therefore? Unless God or language doesn't matter, this is nonsense. Think of some of the changes that might be rung on that sentence: "We believe that child-abuse is an individual decision. And therefore your God-given right." Pro-abortion people would say that because child-abuse involves another individual it is not really an individual decision, but that is exactly the point anti-abortion people want to make; the item at the other end of the decision to abort is not a thing. Never mind, for now. What is fascinating here is what the language really says: because something is an individual decision—as any decision made by any individual is—it is therefore a *right,* even one which has divine sanction. Choice itself is elevated; the very fact that a choice can be made is seen as a thing to be celebrated. And there is something to this. This is what I mean when I say that a pervasive assumption shows through the rhetoric here and reveals a larger, important pattern.

I was talking to a woman who was taking a course on thanatology (the word stripped to its roots, means talk about death) and she was excited by an idea she had encountered in her reading. There ought to be places, she felt, where people could go to commit an "ethical suicide," places where people could end their lives with professional help and without the feeling of guilt. My first reaction to this idea was that I could imagine nothing more desolate than the prospect of looking into the basset-hound eyes of a professional sympathizer during my final moments, and I began to think of the times when I had longed for death—hangovers and long sermons leapt to mind. But I knew that this was making light of an important problem: what about the hard cases, the people whose lives are a continual suffering? Some long and difficult deaths may be exemplary; others are only ugly and seem to mean nothing but pain. What about those who are simply tired of living? Rex Stout, author of the Nero Wolfe books, told an interviewer that his life had been long and good, but he was tired of it. He said that he would like to kill himself, but his relatives wouldn't understand it. As a relatively young man who feels pretty good I can understand what he meant only in an abstract sort of way. But I do find something repellent in the idea of voluntary death chambers for people who decide that they should die, and I tried to tell her what bothered me: maybe suffering has meaning, and our human work is not to impose our own wills on our lives, but to accept what happens to us and try to listen to it, learn from it—this is lame, I know, especially when it comes from someone who is not suffering. But I was also bothered by the fact that a young woman who was every bit as much in the pink as I am was so enthusiastic about the idea of suicide. When I said that even suffering might have some meaning, something to teach us, she said, "Well, dying is a choice. You have a right to make a choice."

The abortion ad and this belief in the right to suicide both assume that choice is not only morally important; choice in itself is made the highest morality. If it can be chosen, it should be permitted. What matters is not what is chosen, but the act of choosing itself.

There is something wrong with this, but also something right. Choice is the thing that makes us human. It is the implications of human freedom which humans most fear, as Dostoevsky shows in *The Grand Inquisitor;* people are eager to avoid those implications. Our freedom is terrifying, and essential. This is the special insight of the modern West, and it is connected with such issues as suicide. In *The Myth of Sisyphus* Camus calls suicide the most important philosophical question. If life is not worth living, if it is meaningless, suicide is consistent with that discovery.

There has been a shift in our perception of freedom of choice and its exercise. At the turn of the century morals were regulated much more strictly than they are today, but manufacturers were quite free to dump poisons into the air and water. The glorious age of capitalism, when poor children could be forced into labor and pollution was the free choice of the plant manager, was finally limited by the community, which realized that some choices are destructive.

Not all choices are equal, obviously. It doesn't matter that we didn't know the damage pollution would do; we live with the consequences of our choice to pollute. But we assume that the area of morality is the only one in the world in which all choices are equally valid.

The moral area is one which is wisely left rather open-ended where legislation is concerned, because in a pluralistic society there is the danger that a dominant ideology or religion will use the power of law to impose its views on people who do not accept them willingly. It is wise to legislate as little as possible. But many of us have come to believe that what is legal is moral, and what is not forbidden is therefore ethically acceptable. This is crazy, but it is one of democracy's weird side effects. Another, related to it, is the belief that all ideas and choices are equal, an idea as shallow as the belief that the will of the majority is always correct and must not be opposed. As a negative insight democracy makes great sense; it keeps some of the most heavy-handed forms of tyranny from taking over completely. As a positive ideology it can be poisonous. It is one thing to say that a person has a legal right to hold whatever stupid ideas he or she wants to hold, because the alternative to allowing this freedom is politically dangerous. It is quite another thing to say that all ideas and choices are in fact equal. We do not make that assumption with regard to pollution, or military spending. Because the results of moral decisions are not easily measured and may forever escape measurement, we act as if they were therefore less real, less important. There is a crude way of assuming that "objective" (i.e., easily quantifiable) data are more real than other data. But there are haunting signs of the limits to this attitude. There are studies, for example, which show that children raised in institutions, without much individual attention or love, are both physically and mentally less developed than other children. This could be seen as an indication that love, which cannot be measured, is nevertheless as real a force as gravity.

Of course you have the right to make choices. But some important questions go along with this: do you have a right to make absolutely any choice at all? Suicide? Abortion? Infanticide? Stupor? At one level, which may or may not be legal (depending on the state's mood) you do, of course. But the questions which are constantly avoided are these: how should we live? Is it good to choose such and such a course? Is it wise? Does it make sense in the light of the fact that we will someday die? If there is a meaning to the fact of our being alive and sentient, will we have blown it if our choices are stupid ones? And, given the right we have to make choices, isn't it possible for us to make truly stupid, wrong-headed, even terrible decisions? Will we be free—as a community, as well as individually—of the consequences of having made our choices? What the law should or should not permit has been made the central feature of a debate which ought to have another focus. What law ought to do is not irrelevant, but spending all of our energy on law is something like worrying about the plumbing, while assuming that a building's architecture will take care of itself.

If there are forces and patterns of meaning which we must discover in order to be human, our culture not only does nothing to encourage our exploring that possibility—it positively discourages it as a serious consideration. Where choice alone is enough, where choice is the ultimate moral category, all of the ways which might be chosen are seen as equal—and equally unimportant.

Feeling Good

"I feel good about myself." A variation: "I'm feeling good about myself now." (This usually comes toward the end of a story about an affair that has ended or a collapsed marriage.)

A close relative to the above: "I'm trying to get in touch with my feelings." The last time I tried to get in touch with my feelings they were out, so I left a note . . .

Well, it does tempt, this sort of language. You look for a trace of humor, and have to conclude that the person who feels bad about himself will, for all his sorry creeping around, make fewer world-class blunders than the person who feels good about himself. The strut always leads to the banana peel, a cosmic law if ever there was one.

I have heard this kind of sentence, and you probably have too, for the past several years, usually from friends whose personal lives are in various states of disarray and who need to get some purchase on things as the ground beneath them turns to swamp. I have also heard it from people who have mild doubts about their own worth and from people who have emerged in one piece from struggles involving divorce, the precarious thing we call "sexual identity" these days, career problems—this "feeling good about myself" is nearly a virus. It seems to be the bottom line in places where guilt used to lurk. Where people once said, "I'm sorry, I acted like a real jerk," now they say "I can't hlep how *you* feel about it—I feel good about myself." Self-love means never having to say you're sorry. There is something finally circular and unanswerable about feeling good about yourself, something neat and sleek, like disco.

There must be more to the feeling than this. It certainly beats hell out of self-loathing, and rightly so: no one should feel bad about his very being—that's too heavy and even foolish a load to carry. In the case of murderers (a couple of whom have admitted to feeling bad about themselves) it seems understandable, but even there it is probably exaggerated, maybe a form of pride. Self-loathing is a kind of hypochondria: it is like listening hard to your heartbeat, convinced that it's going wrong. Self-loathing is a refined narcissism, a backdoor way of paying attention to yourself.

Granting that feeling bad about myself is a bad idea, is its real opposite to be found in feeling good about myself? Two of the people who told me that they felt good about themselves had just seen their marriages collapse not only under themselves but also under their children. Does a "feeling good" declaration amount to a declaration of independence from what has really happened to you, a statement that despite everything you know you can survive? I don't mean to deny the reality of the feeling, which is plainly real; but what can it mean to declare it?

A person who makes it through a period of scary uncertainty intact can find, at the end, a surprising and deep hopefulness. The ability to feel things at all is a proof of life, and it is profoundly refreshing after a bad time. But "feeling good about myself" or "getting in touch with my feelings" can't really help here, because this is the language of alienation, suggesting that I am here, and my self or my feelings are over there, waiting for evaluation or contact. The self, seen as an object among other objects, a thing we can handle and deal with, is a bad idea.

Unfortunately, the self seems to be all we have, especially after faith in everything else has gone: "I feel (good or bad), therefore I am." Now we worry less about what we should do than about how we should feel. Feelings impress us as being more substantial than anything else; in some way they are criteria for judging the importance of what we live through. After disasters reporters stand around the grieving survivors with microphones, and the first question is always, "How did you *feel?*" It is stupid and, given the times, inevitable. Our feelings are our contact with the self—whatever that is. We presume that the self is something we can work on, polishing it into the shape we like; what we want to be is what we are, say the *est* people, and the problem is finding out what we really want.

On a television commercial a woman roars toward me with an expression on her face which would be alarming in any real social circumstance. "I love my new cinnamon-colored hair," she says, nearly dissolving with pleasure, "because it lets me be *me*." In other words, I am what I want to be—that's the best way to be, and it means feeling good about myself. A personality which took this too seriously would finally be insulated from anything outside itself. It was possible for Nazis to feel good about themselves—this was the feeling encouraged by the film *The Triumph of Will*. Self, as a criterion, has a way of forcing everything else out of the picture.

A religious educator told me that the children and adults she worked with suffered from poor self-images. That is too bad, but she felt that she should work at providing good self-images. I disagree. I think we are better off with a less complete scaffolding. A solid sense of self is an idol, according to the desert fathers; Buddhism calls our sense of an enduring self an illusion. If there is anything unanimous in most religious traditions it is the belief that you have to dispense with the self to see the world as it is. A solid sense of self, a self-image, is (like new cinnamon-colored hair) a brittle and silly thing to walk into the world wearing, whether you feel good about it or not.

Deeper Than Emotions

The connection, or lack of one, between our emotions and what we finally are is a mystery which is not on our minds enough. We assume the primary importance of the emotional life to an extent which probably would have seemed strange to our ancestors. (This may be a legacy of Romanticism, which could almost be defined as the range of emotional possibility stretching from *Madame Bovary* to *Dracula*.) We think of the emotions as central to what makes life important. Feeling good about what we are and what we are doing is absolutely important to our consideration of such questions as whether we will continue a marriage or friendship or a line of work. If circumstances, economic or cultural, force us to continue living or working against the emotional grain, we feel that something monumentally unfair is at work in our lives. A strong emotion about a relationship validates it; one which is willed, or which doesn't seem to come from the heart in some way apparent to us, strikes us as false, hypocritical, and somewhat less real.

Emotions do matter and are real, often important, parts of our life. But they are not necessarily guides to how we should live, nor are some of the most overwhelming and apparently good emotions connected with goodness. Deep feelings of love may finally have nothing to do with love in any important sense. Strong emotions may prove no more than indigestion or ulcer symptoms do about the real spiritual state or the virtue of the person who experiences them. Nazis and followers of Pol Pot and members of the Klan all dandle children on their knees. No doubt they have the same visceral feelings about their children that I have about mine: they would die to keep them alive. We know that prominent Nazis were profoundly moved by Bach's music, and it would be a kind of fear, an unreasonable self-protection, for me to assume that what moved them was not the same glory and loveliness that moves me. Torturers no doubt love their wives and children deeply, are loyal to their friends, mourn their dead.

It would be nice if there were some obvious connection between strong affection, powerful emotion, the feelings we believe should make us better people, and the way we really are. It would be nice because it would allow us to believe what we seem to need to believe: that our lives are whole and connected at some level, that we are one sort of being.

But that isn't the case. Given the fact that Nazis can be moved by the emotions of love and loyalty, given the appreciation of beauty which can be found in the soul of the torturer, why is it that this profound feeling does not translate into a feeling about all human beings? How could the love of one parent for his or her child not lead to compassion for all other parents and their children? How could a Mengele happen in the same race which produced a St. Francis of Assisi?

Our age doesn't offer us a good vocabulary for dealing with these things. (This shouldn't lead us to think that other ages were good at them; the fact is that in the ages when officially sanctioned Christianity reigned, it was all right to torment criminals before their death; and of course it was considered permissible to mistreat Jews and schismatics and heretics.) We are tempted to say, "Those people (Nazis, Argentinian torturers, Soviet camp guards, whoever) may feel strongly, but they feel strongly about the wrong things; or they fail to draw the right lessons from what they feel." This presents a new problem: it leads us to the realm of the objective; it leads us to something that can only be called dogma, or orthodoxy.

How does someone come to the "right way" of feeling about something? How is one to know what conclusions are proper? These things don't come from feelings alone; something must be brought to the feeling, some way of reading the feeling which gives us the language we need to say what it means.

The language, for better or worse, comes to us from culture, or religion, or society, but it does come to us from outside; it is not innate. Our fascination with wolf-children, with those who are raised outside of human community, is a reflection of our desire to see what it would be like to see human emotion and response in the raw. Those children will never become Nazis. They lack the language, and therefore presumably the capacity. They will also never become Wallenbergs, or Gandhis, or St. Francises, Bachs, Dostoyevskys, or even ordinarily affectionate and loyal friends or good parents. Maybe in our despair we find ourselves wishing sometimes that this level were as far as humanity could go, the speechless level which would make a murder a local and limited affair, something done only because we have to eat. We have a reasonable, but wrong, fear of the extremes of human freedom. It is wrong to wish to be less than we are capable of being, even if our century makes the wish understandable.

What does this have to do with dogma and orthodoxy? The words have a largely negative reading these days; they suggest a rigidity and closed-mindedness which no one finds sympathetic. Dogma and orthodoxy can be like that, of course. This rigidity exists, however, not only at Jerry Falwell's level or in the claims of the most conservative bishops. It can be found in members of the American Civil Liberties Union and the most liberal Unitarians. What tends to get called "dogmatic" or "orthodox" is unpopular dogma and orthodoxy. (For example, to be pro-choice is not dogmatic; to be pro-life is. It doesn't matter that the same vehemence and closed-mindedness can be brought to either side of the debate.) But dogma means something richer than this.

We can't avoid assuming some things about values and meaning. We assume, for instance, that it is right to pursue justice, even if doing so leads to great personal inconvenience, perhaps to death. There can be no proof for this assumption; it is an *a priori* belief, and one of the few which seems to be shared by a great many otherwise different groups. We may not agree about what justice means, but we do agree that, whatever it means, it is worth risk and inconvenience. We may or may not feel passionate about it, but beyond feeling we understand the need to work for it, even if the work is dogged and without passion. (This could be some of what appeals to us obscurely in the grey atmosphere which surrounds the detective novels of Simenon, Le Carre's thrillers, and it may be why we respond to the stubborn decency of some of Dick Francis's protagonists.) This belief serves as a form of secular dogma: it directs and leads our feelings and emotions, and can transform them.

It would be ideal, our aesthetic sense tells us, if feelings and dogma came together in a case like this and strong emotions meshed with decent belief, forming a whole. But life is frequently not so accommodating. The husband who is faithful to a wife who is terribly ill, acts of courage, friendship in difficult times, all of these can involve going against the emotional grain for the sake of something which we know—even if our knowing is often dim, something truly dark—to be more important than emotion.

Emotions lie at the surface of a perception which is deeper than emotion can ever be. Just as the knowledge of joy is deeper than the emotion of happiness, there are forms of love which are much deeper than the emotions we ordinarily associate with love. It shouldn't be thought that true love involves a steely determination and no feeling at all, although there may be times when it does involve this. Finally, it is a perception, a vision, and an understanding. Like so many other experiences, it may not be immediately and fully available to us; it might involve turning around years after the fact, seeing clearly what love has meant in a particular situation for the first time.

At the beginning of the recitation of the Creed in the Orthodox liturgy the priest says, "Let us love one another, so that with one mind we may confess the Father, Son, and Holy Spirit, the Trinity, one in essence and undivided." Love must be present, informing our confession of faith, for our confession to be true; and we will not be able to see what the love we are called to show one another means, unless we see it dogmatically, in the richest sense of the word. It is a dogma—the Incarnation—that tells Christians what love finally means: a freely accepted self-emptying which allows the Giver of life, who already fills the universe, to become manifest.

Bad Thoughts

"Bad Thoughts" meant one thing when I was a boy in St. Agnes Grade School. The phrase didn't mean thoughts of vengeance or murder; it meant thoughts having to do with sex, which were sinful if you "entertained" or "dwelled on" them. Both words, "entertain" and "dwell," had a nice salacious air. I remember an excruciatingly explicit examination of conscience which was read out to us once a month in the sixth grade. It must have been designed to make sure that if you hadn't had a bad thought at the time the reading began, you would certainly have had several by the end. During this exercise we put our heads down on the desk, arms folded for a pillow, eyes closed for privacy, while a list of specific sins was read out—boring for the first four commandments, having to do with idolatry, profanity, missing Mass, servile work on Sunday, and disobedience to parents; then it picked up as we moved through the violent fifth, and got downright interesting as we waded into the sixth: now we got to the meat, as it were. Here we heard about lustful looks, immodest dress, lewd books, impure touches, and with our eyes closed the whole deck of sins took on a detail as intricate as brocade (red brocade, in fact). We had a lull through the seventh and eighth commandments; then there was the ninth, about other people's wives—we all knew what *that* meant—and we heard the wonderful miserly sound of the word "covet." The rest was anti-climatic, and after a prayer to the Holy Spirit we were trotted off to church and into the box, one at a time, where we made the same confessions we had made for months on end. It was always roughly accurate; you learned how to tone down the most shameful things by being a bit modest about them and sandwiching them in between relatively innocuous sins, and if you exaggerated the number of times you had sinned you figured you were automatically covered: God couldn't blame you for confessing *too much.*

Hundreds of thousands of Catholics went through this sort of thing. While we may regard that part of the past with amusement, or loathing, or nostalgia, few of us are sorry that those days have gone forever. Those of us who have remained Catholic despite everything may not regret having gone through what we did (as one writer said a few years ago, it was funky), but I think most of us are happy that our children are not going through the same obsessive, legalistic routines. In the school my children attend, for example, confession is handled with a refreshing difference. The emphasis is less on law, more on reconciliation, and there doesn't seem to be the dread of confession which I remember.

But I think my children may be missing something. I began to wonder what it was when a friend of mine, a Jew, mentioned the fact that almost all of her close friends were either Jews, Catholics, or ex-Catholics. I realized when she said this that the same thing was true of me, and that the friends who didn't fall into those categories tended for the most part to be Southerners.

I confess: that's narrow, parochial in the worst way. It is, nevertheless, true, and the reason could be that Judaism, Catholicism, and being Southern are all "thick cultures," ways of life. If you come from one of those backgrounds you know, among other things, that you are somehow different from other people . . . not better (well, not necessarily) or worse, but certainly different.

I am not about to defend some of the differences. There was a smug sense of superiority to Protestants (identified, during grade school, with public school kids) which was as far from simple decency as it is possible to get, but this was in large part a reaction to *their* assumption of superiority. It has to be remembered that parochial schools were founded because of a deliberate effort on the part of the American public school system to de-Catholicize the children of immigrants. Self-consciousness about being Catholic, and therefore about being different, helped us toward a realization that some ideas and values matter deeply. Stories of saints who had died for the faith let us know that there were times when the stakes were high, and sacrifice would be called for. Of course it frequently got silly, and of course there were oddly enthusiastic teachers, who were more interested in the dreadful details of martyrdom than in the principle being died for — but was it possible, or is it possible, for values to be discussed in any other American system of common education, without the fake democracy insisted upon by some educators? ("I think Socrates was right, but what do *you* think, Billy?") It surely doesn't require the dreadful examination of conscience routine that we were put through, and I am glad that is something my children won't have to suffer; but at least in parochial schools we were able to hear that some things matter to the death.

It may still be there. But when I go into a church and see banners which say things like "Have a Nice Day" or when the kids bring home cards with stylized pictures of wheat and a few unchallengeably pleasant words, something in me yearns for a holy card of St. Lucy bearing her very real looking eyeballs on a plate: now *there's* religion.

What I'm worried about is blandness. It is something nobody ever accused Catholics or Jews or Southerners of before, but it is worth worrying about when you meet people involved in religious education who speak of "input" and "output" and even "throughput." I know they will all die some day, but in the meantime my children are in school. Are they better off hearing from a young priest who worries about getting in touch with his feelings, or from the weird but by God interesting people who believed that the devil was around the corner waiting with a ball bat? I have a strong feeling that

56

the latter scary picture of the way the world works may be closer to the truth. And I have to ask myself if any other culture could have produced the fierce and utterly right anger which the Berrigan brothers and other members of the Catholic left brought to our understanding of the war in Vietnam — could the WASP desire for universal good citizenship accommodate that? I don't think so; you have to come from a tradition which knows that kings can be evil. This culture has also produced a unique self-consciousness: American Catholics have had to think of themselves specifically as Catholic in a way which doesn't happen anywhere else on earth. Since it had never been an established church, and there was no chance of its ever becoming one, American Catholicism had to understand itself from the beginning in a new way, and this contributed immeasureably to the most revolutionary insight of the Second Vatican Council, the understanding that Christianity is among other things a real perception, and not an institution to be defended like a bank or an armory.

When I go to Mass and listen to the flat lack of cadence which characterizes our liturgy, and when I see some of what my children bring home from school, I worry about blandness. But there is hope. My daughter once expressed an encouraging fear, one which seems to me quintessentially Catholic. She was afraid, she said, that she might some day have a vision.

Let Liturgy Be Liturgy

My daughter came home from the Catholic high school she attends with a complaint about a Mass they'd had. "The priest sounded like a bad Shakespearean actor," she said. I know the priest, and she was right on target. Her comment led me to think about what I don't like, and occasionally downright hate, about liturgy. What follows is not a Lefebvrist plea for a return to the good old days. I don't believe there were any good old days, ever. The church started out bad, and the letters of Paul and James make it clear that liturgical abuses got in on the ground floor. What I do not find in many liturgies is something I have found just often enough to miss it. That is a sense of mystery, and the knowledge that in gathering to celebrate the Eucharist we are doing something important, something which calls out to everything in us.

It has been too easy for some defenders of what most of us have to put up with, liturgically, to dismiss the idea of mystery as either obscurantist or a false memory, so it is important to say what I mean. By mystery I do not mean that we are in the presence of mystery when we are in the presence of something unintelligible. Half of the language of adolescents is unintelligible, but none of it is mysterious. And it is not the shift from Latin to the vernacular which caused the problem.

I have been to Eastern Orthodox liturgies in English which communicated more of mystery than Latin ever did.

What I mean by mystery is the consciousness, not so much of "unfathomable depths," but of a fathoming which doesn't end no matter how deep we go. In the sense that we know there is no limit to what we encounter, the Eucharist is unfathomably deep—but not because anything is closed to us. Instead, we encounter here, with limited vision, something unlimited. This can't happen if there is no perceptible difference between the sort of time we spend on the street and the sort we spend during the liturgy. (The term "spending time" is itself interesting; we do spend time when we regard it as something paid out. But a time passed attentively, with absolute alertness, is not exactly spent—it is appreciated, perceived, more than street time is. Spending time isn't far from killing time.)

Arguments have been made that all time is sacred, and that an attempt to make certain times sacred through ritual can blind us to the holiness of the ordinary. But like the argument that "my work is my prayer," this is a half-truth. Of course all time, coming as it does from God, is sacred. The holiness of time isn't in doubt. The problem is that our perceptions are ordinarily too cluttered to allow us an awareness of the holiness of time, and we need the deliberateness of liturgy, the way it has of altering and slowing time down, to remind us. In the moment before the Orthodox canon begins, the choir sings, "Let us, who mystically represent the cherubim, now set aside all earthly care." The prayers at the foot of the altar, with the sense of moving from one sort of time to another, also accomplished this—or anyway gave an opportunity for its accomplishment. Unless we make this effort consciously we are not likely to develop any deep consciousness of the sacredness of time, just as work cannot really be prayer unless a specific time for prayer is taken apart from our ordinary busy-ness.

This sense of moving from street time to sacred time—a movement which can ultimately result in our appreciation of the sacredness of street time—doesn't happen when a priest comes out, says "Good morning," gets a ragged "good morning" in return, and then says quickly "To celebrate this liturgy let's prepare ourselves by calling to mind our need for God" and, pausing just long enough to make silence awkward and not long enough to allow any real space for prayer, he rattles into the next prayer. People start business meetings with this sort of haphazard rapidity, but it is a lousy way to begin a liturgy.

The old Latin liturgy was often sloppy, and I don't miss it. Nor do I miss Gregorian, which I love; the truth is that outside some miserable attempts by parish choirs—and not many of them—the only place I have ever heard it was on records. Pre-Vatican II Catholic music was, in our parish anyway, as bad as the current stuff. I hate "They'll Know We Are Christians By Our Love" and "Let There Be Peace on Earth"—the first sounds like Howdy Doody Indian music and the second like a skating rink ditty—but "Immaculate Mary Our Hearts Are on Fire" was also pretty bad, musically; being famous didn't help it.

The solution is not a return to the old liturgy but rather an appreciation of the fact that we are called by our faith to transformation, something which liturgy ought to assist us in. That means not an affirmation of time, emotion, and language as we ordinarily perceive it, but help in seeing those common elements of our lives in depth, and this demands a radical shift of perspective. When liturgy makes us feel profoundly self-conscious we are moving in the wrong direction. In *Letters to Malcolm* C. S. Lewis wrote that people who object to novelty in liturgy are not being hidebound at all: "They don't go to church to be entertained. They go to use the service or, if you prefer, to *enact* it. Every service is a structure of acts and words through which we receive a sacrament, or repent, or supplicate, or adore. And it enables us to do these things best—if you like, it works best—when through long familiarity, we don't have to think about it. As long as you notice, and have to count, the steps, you are not yet dancing but only learning to dance. A good shoe is a shoe you don't notice. Good reading becomes possible when you need not consciously think about eyes, or light, or spelling. The perfect church service would be one we were almost unaware of; our attention would have been on God.

"But every novelty prevents this. It fixes our attention on the service itself; and thinking about worship is a different thing from worshipping. . . . A still worse thing may happen. Novelty may fix our attention not on the service but on the celebrant. You know what I mean. Try as one may to exclude it, the question 'What on earth is he up to now?' will intrude. It lays one's devotion to waste."

Unless they are sensitive to what liturgy ought to be about, even the nicest priests can fall into the trap of thinking that their job is to put some new spin into the liturgy, giving it some extra pizzaz. One priest I know, a thoroughly decent man, was given for awhile to beginning his liturgy with "The Lord be with you" (as well he might), and when the people replied "And also with you," he said "Thank you"—as if the people replied that way to do him a favor or compliment him; so I once replied to his reply, "You're welcome," greatly annoying my children; but I really did want to see how long we could keep this little colloquy going. In some ways this assumption that liturgy has to be made new every time isn't just bad liturgy but a profound misunderstanding of liturgy's purpose. Liturgy must lead beyond itself; when the celebrant in any ways calls attention to himself or his personality he leads us smack into the surface of liturgy and we can't get beyond it.

Which leads to what my daughter said: the priest who read the words of the liturgy like a bad Shakespearean actor is a man who feels that the words of the Mass can't live without his beefing them up with special emphases and dramatic gestures. The old liturgy at least made it clear that the action being done was being done for the people by someone who, defective as he might be, represented the people as a whole. He wasn't there to charm them. His personality didn't matter one damn bit. There are feelings which lie buried deep beneath our superficial emotions, and in the same way there are aspects of our person which are obscured by attention to personality. Liturgy ought to address those deeper levels.

But on esthetic grounds alone there are good reasons not to regard the liturgy as a kind of play which needs to be beefed up by its actors. Most high school drama embarrasses us; there aren't that many accomplished actors around. Priests who think they must act the liturgy had better be sure they are very good. If they are very good at acting they will still have missed the point about liturgy, but at least they won't be so embarrassing to the rest of us.

Mom & Pop Forgive Them

There are a number of things to be said about the new readings offered for liturgical use by the National Council of Churches, all but one of them negative. That single thing is that the intention was a decent one. According to the *New York Times*, members of the committee which produced the readings felt that "the use of sexually inclusive language in public worship will undergird other efforts for equality between men and women." This fine aim is not advanced by a tin-eared, anti-historical approach to Scripture. Here are some of the versions (it would not be at all accurate to call them translations; they are revisions) offered by the committee:

> *And because you are children, God has sent the Spirit of the Child into our hearts, crying, "God! my Mother and Father!".* . .(Gal. 4:6)
> *For God so loved the world that God gave God's only Child, that whoever believes in that Child should not perish, but have eternal life.* (John 3:16)

In an article in *The Lutheran*, Bishop James R. Crumley, Jr., of the Lutheran Church in America, said of the above version of John's language, "Attempting to avoid pronouns simply illustrates the need for them in the first place." Bishop Crumley also worried that speaking of God as Mother and Father would not show God's asexuality so much as it might imply God's bisexuality. The Lutheran Church in America will not recommend the use of the new lectionary to its churches. Archbishop Iakovos of the Greek Orthodox Archdiocese of North and South America said that these versions do not "reflect the traditions and reverence of the Holy Scriptures."

I have learned (when arguing against usages like "If anyone wants to reserve a seat, they should see the ticket manager") that the issue of gender in language arouses passionate responses. Let me argue against what has been done in this lectionary by moving to another field, one which matters very much to me. I believe that nonviolence is essential to being Christian. Not everyone agrees with that, just as many would not call the feminist cause essential to Christianity. But if any particular moral focus—justice towards women, nonviolence, the needs of the poor—is allowed to force the revision of Scripture or the partial censoring of literature we will lose the kind of memory that matters to poetry and to a deeper understanding of the symbols which move at levels deeper than rationality and ideology.

Gandhi (hardly a violent sort) was inspired by the *Bhagavad-Gita*. Battle is the metaphor which moves that poem, both literal battle—the protagonist wonders whether it is right for him to engage in it—and spiritual struggle. The poem begins,

> *On the field of Truth, on the battle-field of life, what came to pass, Sanjaya, when my sons and their warriors faced those of my brother Pandu? (The Bhagavad Gita,* Tr. Juan Mascaro, Penguin 1962.)

Despite my firm belief in nonviolence I am not sure that this could be better rendered,

> *In the office of Truth, at the committee meeting of life, what came to pass* (etc.)

I don't mean this to be as flippant as the above might make it seem, but some attempts to deal with real problems are so insensitive to other questions, and to the limitations of our own age's understanding, that if taken seriously they will lead us into a set of problems at least as thorny as the ones we are trying to solve. To take one example, gutting the Old Testament of its most violent scenes, or bowdlerizing them to make them less violent, has resonances which move more deeply than the question we hope to address when we move in with the editor's pencil. Moses lifts his arms at God's command for victory, and when he lowers them in weariness his army begins to lose; when they are raised again, propped up by his companions, the army begins to win. At its most superficial level this is an important metaphor about prayer, and it goes even deeper than that.

I kneel in churches, when kneeling is called for, and in social circumstances find myself shaking hands. Both of these rather common symbols have their roots in war. Kneeling puts you in a physically vulnerable position before a superior who can kill you, now that you aren't on your feet and able to maneuver. A handshake means putting you sword hand into the hand of another, whose sword hand is held by yours: you keep one another from striking. This is at once a sign of peace, in its most negative and limited form, and of peace's vulnerability. It is not at all a sign of peace's fullness, but is rooted in the fragility of worldly peace. It comes to us from the ancient history of the West, and in all its limitation is full of peaceful meaning.

The language of Scripture is in some ways comparable. No one I know imagines that God is physically male. But is this all that the language of Scripture means in referring to God as Father? Is another primitive and complicated level of metaphor at work in symbols which involve sex? We speak of "mother earth," and mean a recurrent fertility which happens naturally and rhythmically.

The mother was a symbol of fertility, oasis-like, and the womb and the navel were signs of our return to that source. Fatherhood did not have that necessity or earthiness about it. Without entering into the complicated question of which symbol is the better one for expressing our relationship to the divine (my feeling is that we need both, as Julian of Norwich knew when she referred to divine motherhood), it could be that God seen as Father is necessary in moving symbolically towards the idea of creation from nothing, a creation which *did not need to be.* Symbols are not simply reduced, and they are dealt with simply only by high school English teachers and those ideologically inclined folk—I really don't care what their causes are, how good or how bad or how silly—who think that we can make the world over with mind and force, as if we were ruled primarily by reason and that tiny part of the imagination we are aware of. There are vaginal and phallic symbols all over the mythical landscape, especially the Hindu part. The magician's wand is phallic, and so is the Easter candle plunged into the waters of the baptismal font, which is plainly womblike. To reduce sexual symbols to tokens which we trade in crude exchanges about power and economic equality is to miss much that symbols have to tell us. I wouldn't for a moment claim that those symbols have nothing at all to do with power and equality, or that their evolution wasn't influenced by some very ugly factors.

But the *more* which is involved where there is more to it than that is very important—even of the essence. The weirdness involved in being human is that we are at once ape and angel. We are gifted and cursed with teeth and claws and instincts which pull at us from where we have been and push us towards what we will be. It would not be a human improvement to file down our canine teeth because of what they imply about what we have come from. To deny or forget that origin is dangerous. It is also not only dangerous but foolish to see it as simply bad, bad as it may often have been. A religion which has become an anti-idolatrous form of monotheism (what a dreadful way to talk about the living God, but here we are, impaled on a language) does in fact have patriarchal origins. Like the handshake, or the grin which reveals canine tooth, the language of Scipture tells us what we have come from and points the way to what we will be. It is part of incarnation, of being flesh and having a long history. It should not be rewritten to prop up a less carnal, and therefore less historical and finally less real, picture of ourselves.

Religion & Reflex

I was in an Orthodox church in a small southern Illinois coal town when a middle-aged woman came in, crossed herself, kissed the icon at the end of the aisle, and walked back to a pew. Her gesture had the swift and easy quality I have seen in Catholic churches when people enter, touch the water in the font and cross themselves as they move to their pews. Although I have attended only a few synagogue services, I have noticed the same combination of inattention and ritual taken seriously. In some people these gestures, done as a repeated part of spiritual observance, smooth out over the years until they become stylized, one flow like the line at the edge of a piece of driftwood.

There is something now which makes us uncomfortable around such traditional practices, with their ancient and familiar mix of prayer, attention, devotion, habit, inattentiveness, and lack of self-consciousness. Maybe this is apparent only to someone whose liturgical experience is as varied as that of my generation (which is to say, those of us who are in our late thirties or early forties). When I entered college the Mass was in Latin. My children have relatively little connection with the church of my childhood. At any rate, there is a self-consciousness which comes of this experience which makes us self-conscious even about self-consciousness. The woman in the Orthodox church made me wonder about religions in the industrialized West these days (as a columnist it is my job to soar in this way from the particular to the grand) and about what we may be losing.

What we are losing is the lack of self-consciousness, a lack which drives some people crazy whenever they encounter traditional religion or popular religious devotion. "Don't these people pay any attention to what they are doing? Do they think these repeated actions will save them?" That sort of complaint isn't uncommon. A lot of Catholic liberals and fundamentalist Protestants are embarrassed by the old lady who moves her lips when she says her prayers, or by signs of the cross which are done rapidly and which seem to the non-participant's eye to be simply careless. What we need, the embarrassed objectors seem to say, is a little self-consciousness. I have seen that self-consciousness at liturgical conferences where people learn to bow from the waist rather than genuflect when they enter a church, and so they do so as they approach the altar, very carefully and properly, having learned just that afternoon.

There is, however, a lack of precisely this self-consciousness which is the mark of moving more deeply into religious observances. It is when you don't have to think of something that you have learned it. Toddlers think about walking much more than we do; they pay lots of attention to it. The point of such gestures as the sign of the cross is, among other things, the participation of the body as well as the mind in prayer. That includes automatic reflexes, habits, all of the non-rational things which remind us that we are not in control. As long as the mind insists on being the most important part of all this (as it does when we assume that an automatic gesture is worthless because we haven't thought about what we were doing—would this be true if I waved a fly away from my eyes thoughtlessly, or closed them reflexively against lye?), to that extent the body's place in the relationship which is implied by prayer—one which has to do with everything about us—is discounted.

But more than the body's place in prayer is involved in this difference between traditional forms of religion and a self-consciousness which marks more recent forms of devotion. My son was recently confirmed. As part of the preparation for confirmation the parents of the children to be confirmed were expected to send a letter to the school telling our children how much we loved them, and how proud of them we were. A number of parents sat down and dutifully wrote letters, and I have no doubt that sincere things were said and that some children and parents were moved. But what bothered me about the whole attempt was this: what does this do to spontaneous expression of feeling? It may be that there are children whose parents do not tell them what they feel for them, parents who are reluctant to show any overt affection at all, and that is sad. I come from a family where people kiss a lot and where, especially late at night after family gatherings have settled out a bit, brothers and sisters can talk for hours about what's right and wrong with all of us. I think it's a good thing that we are able to do this, and it is precisely because it is good that I would hate to see it made into a form of homework. If I have to be told to love my child, or my wife, something is wrong; these things aren't there to be evoked on cue. It is not a sign of love or of natural feeling when these things are assigned, but of the death of real feeling. The assignment is the symptom of a problem and is not even close to being a cure.

There is in this sort of assigned emotion an equation of religion and therapy. If parents and children do have a problem communicating their love for one another (or worse, if they don't have any love to communicate), the problem is not remedied by self-consciousness about it during the preparations which surround a sacramental occasion. Not that the sacraments have nothing to do with love—of course they do, with human as well as divine love. But deep problems in this area require individual pastoral attention, not wholesale attempts to evoke feeling. What is being sought in the sort of assignment my son was given is, of course, not a bad thing: it is good for children to know that their parents love them. But what was also being sought was a moving experience; I have seen the same thing gone after in other liturgies. This has as little to do with Christianity as the deep swoons of Victorian teenagers reading romantic novels.

This sort of thing—an organized, self-conscious experience—increasingly takes the place of forms of devotion which have fallen out of our lives. You may have had a different experience of this than I have, but I don't know many children who are really enthusiastic about any of these exercises (I don't know any, in fact); and although we were bored by such things as the Stations of the Cross during Lent, we didn't think they were corny. My children, without any coaching from me, have expressed that feeling about much of what they are exposed to in the name of religion. They know when someone is trying to move them. They have, after all, lived through a lot of Bell Telephone and Coke commercials.

The equation of religion with good feelings and the attempt to evoke those feelings doesn't go as deeply as some old and now ignored devotions did. I don't know the solution to this problem—can those older forms be restored at this point?—but it is a problem indeed, and a couple of things I have read during the past year make me wonder about it. In the important *Journal of Religion in Communist Lands* published by Keston College (Heathfield Road, Keston, Kent BR2 6BA, England) there was an account of a mass pilgrimage to a Catholic shrine near Shanghai. The church which was the goal of the pilgrims had been shut during the Cultural Revolution; it was forcibly reopened by the pilgrims, who prayed there for hours. (Many of them were fishermen, and gave space on their boats for fellow pilgrims to sleep while they prayed.) Holy objects—pictures, rosaries—and common recited prayers were a central part of this. Another article in the same issue tells of the Yugoslav government's irritation with an alleged Marian apparition in that country. These incidents made me think of the important place the Black Madonna occupies in Poland, and the hope which Guadalupe has brought to millions of poor Mexicans. It is significant that this sort of devotion and such things as common recited prayers and litanies play such an important part in the survival of faith during hard times. Do we have any equivalents? Will our children?

Man Becomes God

During every Christmas season someone feels obliged to point out from the pulpit that Christmas is not the greatest Christian feast. Easter and Pentecost were both considered more important in the ancient church, because they celebrated the Resurrection — which was, after all, the point of Jesus's life — and the birth of the church which is charged with spreading the gospel. A variation on this scrooge-ish line is the reminder that Christmas didn't happen exactly as we think it did, that the infancy narratives are instructive fables, and so forth. Not that I would quarrel with the truth of what gets said in such homilies; but there does seem to be a joylessness in people for whom such sterile considerations are important. They are like the English professors who ask questions like "What do you think Yeats meant when he has the narrator mention the fire in his head?"

Stories and poems are as real as coral reefs, and their meanings are not simply detachable. The person who can speak easily of the Resurrection as a "faith event," or some equivalently slimy term, and who locates its meaning within the Christian community's reading of that event (leaving the datum on which the belief was based in a limbo which apparently doesn't matter), looks to most believers and non-believers like someone embarrassed at being caught in a tradition which has at times been able to speak, without hedging, as if it really did believe what it says it believes. Of course the conservative who regrets the absence of a photographer at the tomb entrance is just as tone-deaf. Both seem to want God to

71

conform, to fit into patterns their views demand. Their faith is in *their faith,* and as such it doesn't matter; it also misses so much of what the story, as a story, has to say.

The fact is that despite everything said to turn them in other directions, Western Christians *like* Christmas better than any other feast. If Christmas, over several centuries came to be an important feast, it is worth wondering what such a slowly dawning thing has to tell us. The Irish writer Noel Dermot O'Donoghue has written of "the depths of which dogma is the surface." Dogma, and the stories which give it birth, attend it, and grow around it through time, point us in the direction of a reality so deep that no story (and certainly no dogmatic formulation) can exhaust it.

Until the fifth century there was no agreed-upon date for the celebration of Jesus's birth. It was not considered as important as the feast of Epiphany, which (because it was the sign of Jesus's revelation to the world) was commonly believed to be more central to Christian faith than the celebration Jesus's physical birth. Origen opposed the celebration of Christmas, which he found too much like the pagan custom of celebrating the births of kings and pharaohs. There were other pagan associations as well. An argument once advanced for celebrating the feast during the spring makes Christmas sound like a fertility rite: since the world was created in a springlike, blooming state, Christmas, the birth of the world's true life, must be in the spring. Bede writes that before the arrival of Christianity in England, the 25th of December was celebrated as "mother's night," and it involved an all-night vigil. Pagan emblems like the evergreen were borrowed for the feast.

The pagan influences are interesting enough to suggest to some writers that the feast of Christmas grew from a need to woo pagans from their own feasts, leaving them with enough of the old ways to content them, while sliding in the Christian message on the sly — the sugar around the pill, so to speak. Without denying that there might be some truth in this, it should be pointed out that it is much too simple a notion. In fact, pagan elements were usually condemned at first, and were reluctantly accepted only when it became clear after several generations that, condemned or not, some of the old ways were going to stay.

The other overlooked fact is that Christmas grew in importance not so much to fight off paganism but to fight off another version of Christianity. Christmas was the feast of the Word made flesh, an emphasis which had been obscured by the adoptionism which saw Jesus's divinity as something conferred upon him at his baptism. The Christmas feast affirmed the holiness of the flesh, flesh "chosen before time began," as adoptionism never could. And while there is a point to Origen's worry that Christmas celebrations were suspiciously like the pagan celebrations of kingly birth, the celebration of Jesus's birth and the stories which surround it, with all their scenes of poverty and exile, turn the conventional notion of kingship upside down. (In this the feast is like the early Christian affirmation "Jesus is Lord," a deliberate counter to the Roman "Caesar is Lord.") This king "came not to be served but to serve," and his reign began in a stable.

The radicalism of the Incarnation might seem to have been domesticated by our way of making Christmas a simply jolly feast, but some of its harsh and unsentimental aspect has always showed through, for example in the traditional carol "What Child Is This?" It contains the words, "Good Christians, fear. For sinners here the silent Word is pleading... Nails, spears shall pierce him through..." The joy of a child's birth and the tragedy of his later suffering were associated from the first.

No Christian feast can finally be separated from the others. The Word made flesh, born on Christmas, rose from the dead on Easter. If Christians have, over the centuries, made Christmas an important feast it might be because of the closeness of the event to ordinary experience. It is, to say the least, difficult to imagine rising from the dead. But nearly everyone has experienced the birth of a child in some way, and this commonness brings the feast close to home. At the same time, the assertion that there is something divine about this child, that the strange story of Incarnation begins in this universal human circumstance — this is what makes Christmas at once the most accessible and radical feast. No other feast expresses the paradox of Christianity better: the God who came in the vulnerable and needy form of a child is very much a part of the tradition which includes Abraham's dark obedience, the crucified Christ, and the God who makes himself bread to be eaten.

However, this notion of Incarnation can stop too easily at sentimentality. The Word did not become flesh just in order to move us or bring tears to our eyes annually. One ancient implication of the doctrine of Incarnation has been neglected in recent years; Christmas is a good time to reflect on what the Fathers of the church called *deification,* the belief that we are meant to share in divinity, and that anything less is less than Christianity. Paul called Jesus "the first born" of many brothers and sisters, and in the gospel of John Jesus asks the Father "that the love you had for me may be in them, and I may be in them." Jesus, according to the Fathers, is the image of what each of us is meant to be. The important distinction was not between Jesus's divinity and our humanity; rather, Jesus's divine humanity was his by nature, and ours was a gift.

This is, of course, a hard saying. It is so unsettling that many theologians find it hard to hear its implications at all. In his book *On Being a Christian* Hans Kung asks of deification, "But does a reasonable man *today* want to become God? What were stirring patristic slogans at that time — like 'God became man so that man might become God' — are almost completely unintelligible today. The theme of an exchange between God and man (or between the two 'natures'), highly relevant for Hellenistic hearers, means nothing at all to an age so sensitive as ours to the absence of God and 'God's darkness.' Our problem today is not the deification but the *humanization of man.* Even in the New Testament what happened in and with Jesus of Nazareth is not interpreted everywhere as an incarnation of God or — more exactly — of God's son or God's Word. If this interpretation is to have any meaning at all for modern man it will only be in virtue of its implications for man's becoming man." (*On Being a Christian,* Doubleday, pp. 442-443)

Hans Kung has done so much valuable work (especially in combating certain unChristian notions of infallibility and ecclesiastical franchises on God's truth) that it seems picky to mention what is wrong with this passage; but has anyone ever seriously suggested that the Fathers believed deification to be intelligible? Or that intelligibility is the point? The reference to "modern man," "reasonable men today," "our problem today," and "an age so sensitive as ours" all perpetuate the notion of modern enlightenment vs. previous darkness. No one reasonable wants to become God, but this is due partly to the fact that as we are *now* we cannot really know what or who God is; we do not know what becoming God would mean. That is part of the point. Gregory Nazianzen said that those who attempted to pry into the mystery of God would go mad, and Basil said that anyone who claimed to know God was depraved. No serious theologian or mystic of any age has been unaware of the absence or darkness of God, though in our time of Hiroshima, the Holocaust, and universal boredom it is no longer the theoretical preserve of theologians, but an omnipresent reality.

It is true, as Hans Kung says, that this doctrine has a meaning if it can speak to us of what it means to become truly human. I would suggest, though, that it is not enough to use words like "humane" or "humanization" without reference to deification. The reason that we cannot at present know what God is is that we are in the idol-making business: even God becomes an idol. We cherish the image of God, the notion of what it means to be Christian, a picture of the church; and all of them stand in the way of God, the life of Christ, and true Christianity. To ask for intelligibility is, I think, a mistake. God at work in us may seem to be absolute emptiness (as God was to Abraham, Job and Jesus in Gethsemane); but it is this emptiness at work in us which can uncover the divine humanity, and it is this which defines the truly human, rather than anything we can arrive at on our own.

Not quite to prove the point, but nearly, let me offer an example of human self-definition worked up by someone less profoundly informed than Hans Kung (who, working from a tradition which has accepted the belief in deification, correctly identifies many of our false gods). In *Self-Esteem* (Celestial Arts Press) Virginia Satir writes, "I am me. In all the world there is no one else exactly like me. Everything that comes out of me is authentically mine because I alone choose it. I own everything about me — my body, my feelings, my mouth, my voice. . . . I own all my triumphs and successes, all my failures and mistakes. Because I own all of me I can become intimately acquainted with me. By so doing I can love me and be friendly with me in all my parts. . . . Whatever I think and feel at a given moment in time is authentically me. If later some parts of how I looked, sounded, thought and felt turn out to be unfitting, I can discard that which is unfitting, keep the rest, and invent something new. . . . I own me, and therefore I can engineer me. I am me, and I am OK.''

This is a pathetic example of what happens when traditional wisdom is lost, and traded away for "going to where the people really are" (to use a current catch-phrase in religious education). Where they really are is in some kind of shopping center, being victimized, more than anything else, by a society which sees everything as controllable, potentially understandable, with happiness and fulfillment a goal and a right, rather than an occasional, fortuitous thing — a world with no unpredictable or uncontrollable limits.

The radical belief expressed at Christmas is that the source of everything sent his own life into flesh because of love, and shares that life with us. A doctrine of Incarnation which does not go as far as the Fathers did in asserting our own divine humanity can become idolatrous: Jesus becomes another remote god, and not the God who emptied himself to share humanity. If modern man does not understand a statement like "God became man so that man might become God" this is only because no one understands it. It can be lived only by emptying ourselves of all our notions of God and man. The symbols which surround the story of Christmas are upsetting ones: a pregnant virgin gives birth to a child in a barn, and the child is the world's salvation. The story of the Incarnation, and the ancient belief in deification, might show us that it is not enough to aim at being human. It is better to begin with our unknowing, spending what might be a confusing and dark time in the presence of someone presently unknowable, in order to find out what we are called to be.

The Reality of Easter

"I was once, five or six years ago, taken by some friends to have dinner with Mary McCarthy and her husband, Mr. Broadwater... Toward morning the conversation turned on the Eucharist, which I, being the Catholic, was obviously supposed to defend. Mrs. Broadwater said that when she was a child and received the Host, she thought of it as the Holy Ghost, He being the 'most portable' person of the Trinity; now she thought of it as a symbol and implied that it was a pretty good one. I then said, in a very shaky voice, 'Well, if it's a symbol, to hell with it.' That was all the defense I was capable of but I realize now that this is all I will ever be able to say about it, outside of a story, except that it is the center of existence for me; all the rest of life is expendable."

This passage from *The Habit of Being,* Sally Fitzgerald's wonderful collection of Flannery O'Connor's letters, came to mind recently when I was trying to figure out what bothered me about some approaches to scriptural interpretation and Christian doctrine. If the danger of conservative Christianity is its tendency towards legalism and fundamentalism, the danger of liberal Christianity is a kind of embarrassment before the claims of traditional Christianity. What we wind up with is pretty thin soup. I understand why we are offered this diet; it is easy to see what it is meant to remedy. As an alternative to fundamentalism, however, it is not only not adequate; it is hardly interesting.

There are interpretations of the resurrection, for example, which bypass the question of whether Jesus actually rose from the dead in order to consider the state of mind of the early church. The resurrection mattered to the faith of the apostles, according to this line of thought, and it is this faith which counts, not whether or not the event happened in time. The importance of the resurrection is to be found in the "faith experience" of the church.

It is almost an embarrassment to bring up the question of the empty tomb to someone who urges this point of view; you feel like Lenny in *Of Mice and Men*: "Tell me about the rabbits, George." But the belief that Jesus really rose has been central to Christianity. A strictly fundamentalist view of this doctrine may lead us to overlook some of the lessons the doctrine is meant to teach us; plainly the main significance of the resurrection is not the fact of a resuscitated corpse. Here some words of Simone Weil are brutally to the point: Hitler could rise from the dead a thousand times, she said, and she would never believe that he was the son of God. A miracle can be seen for what it is only where there is a prior faith, able to receive it; it would never convince someone simply as an historical or physical fact. To this extent what counts is the faith of the church, and not what a camera placed at the entrance of the tomb might reveal. Insisting on too literal an approach can make us less sensitive to the need for faith.

However, there is a way of talking about the resurrection which avoids fundamentalism by speaking of the way Jesus was, after his death, alive "in the lives of his disciples." Sounds pretty dead to me. There is something watery and insipid about this approach to the "faith experience" of the early church; it reminds me of the sort of thing liberal ministers who wanted to uplift everyone and offend no one used to trot out: "Those great men of history, Roosevelt, Gandhi, Lincoln, Jesus, and Plato. . . ." Intense experiences are a dime a dozen. They aren't enough to base a life on, especially not one which might take you to death, where experiences end for good. If Jesus lived only as any impressive dead person lives, there is no more reason to be a Christian than there is to be a Platonist.

What is clear from Scripture, from the testimony of the early church, and what has been believed by orthodox Christians throughout history is that a man who was killed lived again, not as a ghost or as an appearance of his former self, but as someone alive with a new kind of life. He appears sometimes as a stranger, recognized "in the breaking of the bread" or in serving breakfast to his friends, who had gone back to their trade as fishermen and were hungry after a night of fruitless work. It is that mysterious one we should look to, realizing that whatever it was that happened at the resurrection it transcended all ordinary categories of experience, including the merely factual or historical.

Some interpretations of Scripture are resented not because they aren't fundamentalist enough, but because they offer a vision which doesn't look as rich or as comprehensive as the traditional sort. People understandably do not feel that they have found the pearl of great price when told they should move away from the question of whether a man really rose from the dead to a consideration of the state of mind of the early church. This is not only hopelessly academic; it isn't even the right way to tell a story.

What I think we are faced with is a fear of the marvelous. We are too time-bound, too prejudiced in favor of the categories acceptable to educated, middle-class modern Western white folks to consider the possibility that there really is such a thing as the miraculous, the marvelous, the uncanny, the supernatural. We want to explain Christian faith in terms which won't offend people to whom the idea of a miracle is scandalous (as if it weren't scandalous to first-century pagans, who considered Christians a credulous lot). Maybe this can't be done. Maybe the Western worldview which has prevailed since the Enlightenment is too limited, and needs shaking up with stories of multiplied loaves and fishes, transfiguration, and resurrection. In her excellent book *The Passionate God* (Paulist) Rosemary Haughton brings a wider vision to bear on the mystery of the Incarnation; anyone tired of thinner stuff should turn to Haughton's refreshing theology.

There have been some people about whom fantastic stories have been told. Only fantastic stories could tell the truth about them. They include not only Jesus, but Saint Francis of Assisi and the founder of Hasidism, the Baal Shem Tov. It is interesting that our first question about them is, "Why would people tell a story like that, unbelievable as it is," rather than "What if things like that could happen? What would that tell us about the sort of world we live in?" (One thing it tells us is that the world is not the safe, predictable place we thought it was.) The mysterious is a real dimension of human experience. It is made no less real by the fact that our culture isn't very good at dealing with it.

Is God Indifferent?

There have been questions about the mystery of evil and the goodness of God ever since Job and before, and some philosophers have separated the types of evil into "natural" and "human" evil: natural evil is the suffering caused by earthquakes, cancer, and death; human evil is involved in unkindness, war, and the horror of concentration camps. The argument against God has been put succinctly: If God is God he is not good; if God is good he is not God. "God" here means some omnipotent being who arranges everything that happens.

No one can take the question lightly. Or rather, it can be taken lightly or considered of academic interest until it comes close, and then it becomes important in a visceral way. Recently we have encountered one example of suffering after another. My youngest sister's first child died in her womb only days before it was to have been delivered. The brother of one of my closest friends—his only living relative—was paralyzed in a swimming accident and is alive only because of surgery, a pacemaker, and a respirator; he will spend what is left of his life that way. It is impossible sometimes not to be angry at the way the world is, which means at the very least that we direct some tough questions towards God—or if not towards God, towards our ordinary beliefs about God. It is easy to have some sympathy for those gnostics who believed that the God who created the physical universe is deranged or evil, and the good God is somewhere else.

But I can't believe that. There are too many other things true about the world. An infant's growth in understanding is part of the same physical world which sees the death of other infants. Friendship is as possible as war, and happens more often. The same physical laws which can make undertow murderous and sink ships are also at work in the logarithmic spiral which makes the shell of the chambered nautilus as beautiful as anything Bach ever wrote. I can't love the beauty of the chambered nautilus (or of Bach's Brandenburg concertos) and believe that the God who created the universe in which such things can happen is deranged.

But indifferent? That's the stronger temptation. The skies over Auschwitz were silent. Stars moved through them and clouds made lovely patterns. The existence of such a horror moves us to despair of any goodness—if not of God's, certainly of humanity's. But Auschwitz was something human beings did to other human beings. In a way it serves more to reveal human than divine evil—which only postpones the question: why were we made capable of such things? There is something to the argument that we are not free unless we are free even to be demonic; but that argument is offered easily too often. It is tempting to think of God as utterly indifferent to humanity; it is tempting to try to echo in our own hearts what Camus called "the sublime indifference of the universe." Loving other people hurts us, because we must witness them being hurt and finally dying. To detach yourself from pain is possible and tempting, but the price is terrible. We know that if we love people we will suffer, but if we refuse to love them we are dead on our feet, animate corpses. Better to be hurt than to be impervious to the pain love will inevitably bring us to.

Suffering and love are connected somewhere too deep for us to see. There are times when love shows itself in suffering, and is revealed in a way we don't see in other places. One couple I know suffered through the slow death of their child. Their response was a staggering generosity to other suffering children and their parents.

A few weeks ago we had dinner with a couple who have been through an extraordinary amount of suffering. The husband was treated for Hodgkins disease. After radiation treatment the illness abated for nearly five years; in those days they called five years a cure. He had just been engaged when the disease returned. A debilitating round of chemotherapy treatments fought the disease off again, and he has been in remission for, I think, about ten years. During that period his youngest brother died in an accident, and his wife developed malignant melanoma. She was treated successfully and has been well for a couple of years. This would be enough to crush anyone. This is what has happened: my friend was told that as a result of radiation treatment he might not be able to father a normal child. He and his wife waited until tests showed that everything seemed to be all right, and they now have a child.

He's a glorious kid in his own right, but this loving willingness, the love and hope he represents, the good news that he *is* in a family which has known such suffering, makes him a kind of miracle baby. He is a sign of the goodness which is part of the world we suffer in.

There are times when suffering makes us believe that if God can be said to love human beings, it isn't a love which bears any relationship to what human beings call love. This makes sense, but it might be more to the point to say that if God is all-powerful, it is not power as human beings understand it. We think of power as manipulation, force, coercion, and the imposition of authority. But if the power of God is at one with God's love, it may be reflected in those instances of love which suffering reveals. And we can hope for the faith which can believe that the love revealed there is stronger and more enduring than the horrible suffering which makes it apparent.

Finally nothing can solve the problem of evil. (Can we imagine any explanation which would allow us to say, "Ah! That makes the suffering of children all right, then. Sorry I didn't catch on sooner.") Our endless questioning and even our anger at God make more sense than easy attempts to deal with something as terrible as human affliction. At the end of the book of Job, God reproaches Job for his questions. But in the epilogue, which is thought to be of later composition, God reproaches Job's comforters for their easy attempts to explain away Job's questions: "You have not spoken truthfully about me as my servant Job has done." The tacked-on ending to Job has been maligned for restoring Job's fortunes and for trying to turn Job into a book with a happy ending, but the belief that Job's anguished questions were appropriate is also underscored here, and it is essential. No approach to suffering is worse than the one which tries to make suffering less than it is. I remember from childhood a pious attempt to make Jesus's words "My God, my God, why have you forsaken me?" a pious quote from the psalms, and a reproach to his crucifiers. The teacher who offered this explanation was at pains to assure us that Jesus did not *really* feel abandoned. She said nothing about the account of his agony at Gethsemane, where we are told his soul "was filled with dismay and dread," and his prayer that he be spared suffering was (as several writers have pointed out) the only prayer in the New Testament which was not granted.

Orthodoxy:
The Third Way

A typical presentation of Christian belief divides the Church into Catholic and Protestant branches. There are, of course, more subtle distinctions to be made, but Catholicism and Protestantism are commonly understood to be poles of Christianity, with the worship and belief of any given denomination tending towards one or the other. When fundamentalist preachers exhort their audiences to attach themselves to "Bible-believing churches" it is clear what they are trying to distance themselves from. When Episcopalians or Lutherans speak of a "liturgical church" they are moving in the other direction. Most of us grew up with an even more cut-and-dried picture — we were members of the One True Church, founded on Peter, divided by an apostate monk at the time of the Reformation; or we were part of the tradition which after centuries of intolerable decadence managed to rescue the Word of God from the authoritarian Roman cabal.

Now we are more charitable. Protestants worry more than they once did about what was lost at the Reformation, and Catholics recognize what was gained there. But both Protestant and Catholic traditions are in crisis now. Neither seems to address the condition of many of our contemporaries, who are not really opposed to Christianity — they are simply indifferent to it.

There is a third kind of Christianity which could offer the West a perspective it badly needs in these dry times. The Eastern Orthodox Church is still largely unknown to Western

Christians, and where it is known it is frequently misunderstood. Orthodoxy is viewed as a kind of "Catholicism without the Pope," a static, archaic collection of national churches which somehow fell out of step with the rest of Christian history. A first glance doesn't do much to correct this impression: many American Greek and Russian churches seem to be baptized ethnic clubs, and the fact that Orthodox bishops in America have ethnic, rather than regional, jurisdiction reinforces the image of Orthodoxy as nationalistic, non-papist Catholicism (despite the fact that the American situation is deplored by most Orthodox theologians, and is actually a violation of Orthodox canon law).

The Russian theologian Khomiakov wrote: "All Protestants are crypto-Papists. To use the concise language of algebra, all the West knows but one datum a; whether preceded by the positive sign $+$, as with the Romanists, or with the negative $-$, as with the Protestants, the a remains the same."

This, like much of Khomiakov's polemical anti-Romanism, is something of an exaggeration. But his essential point is that much of Christian history in the West has been intimately involved with the consolidation of Papal power, and with reactions to it. Because of this Western preoccupation, Western interpretations of Orthodoxy usually begin and end with observations about the similarity of Orthodoxy to Catholicism or to Protestantism. However, much more than papal power is involved in the differences between Orthodoxy and the West. Orthodoxy presents us with a vision of Christianity which is full of apparent contradictions: it is hierarchical, but remarkably democratic; ascetic but not legalistic; conservative and flexible; and at the center of this vision is a belief that humanity shares in the transfiguration of Jesus, that we are called on to be divine.

The differences between Eastern and Western Christianity go back to early Church disagreements about the authority of bishops. Five bishops — known as Patriarchs — were pre-eminent, because the cities in which they resided had unusual religious or political importance. Antioch, Alexandria, and Constantinople were important centers of imperial power, as was Rome; Jerusalem's importance was religious. In addition, Peter had been bishop in Antioch as well as Rome, where Peter and Paul were both martyred. Following the fall of Rome the Church was divided along Eastern and Western lines, with the former imperial authority shifted East and the Church in the West isolated from the other major Church centers. The authority of the bishop of Rome was the only authority which remained intact through the crisis in the West, and the Pope found himself the continuing sign of unity with the Roman as well as the Christian past. The Church of Rome had long been the first Church in the Christian world, not only because it was situated in the imperial capital but also because it was the city in which the two chief apostles of the Church were martyred, and Peter had founded the Church there. When there were quarrels between other churches, Rome was frequently called on for arbitration. There is a good deal of evidence that this primacy was one of honor, not absolute jurisdiction. Quarreling churches usually accepted the Roman verdict, but did not have to. The role of the Pope in these disputes was not that of ruler, but reconciler; he was a sign of the Church's unity.

As the separation of the Western Church from the Eastern Churches continued, the role of Pope and Patriarch began to change. Rome argued that it had jurisdiction over the other churches. The other patriarchs argued that while the Pope was certainly the first among equal brothers, his primacy was honorific and not juridical. In time Rome began to base its case on the words of Jesus to Peter: "You are Peter, and upon this rock I will build my Church." The Orthodox bishops argued that the Roman interpretation could not be found in the writings of the Fathers of the Church, who intended to agree that Jesus' words referred to Peter's confession, immediately preceding them: "You are the Christ, the Son of the Living God." This confession was the basis of the Church, and applied to every Christian. In a more restricted sense the authority given to Peter was given to every bishop, to everyone whose authority derived from Peter, and while in the West it was impressive to argue that the Pope was Peter's successor, since Peter was bishop of Rome, it was less impressive in the East, since Peter was also bishop of Antioch. Added to this was the fact that while there were references to Rome's special place in some early Christian writers, the primary stress was on the authority of the bishop, who was at the center of every church. In 1054, following centuries of disagreement, Pope Leo IX's emissary excommunicated Michael Cerularius, the Orthodox patriarch of Constantinople, who in turn excommunicated the papal legate and everyone in his party. Contact between the Eastern and Western branches of the Church continued, however strained, until Islamic Crusaders took over many formerly Orthodox areas of the East, and when Catholic crusaders — whose mission was ostensibly the rescue and aid of Christians — sacked the Orthodox city of Constantinople, the rift between the competing traditions was sealed.

It is clear that many cultural and political factors were involved in the schism. There are also doctrinal factors which can't be minimized. One, obviously, was the growing Roman belief in the papacy's absolute authority. Another, related to the first, was a dispute over a phrase in the Nicene Creed. The bishops gathered at the Council of Nicaea had gone to the gospel of John for the words describing the Holy Spirit, "who proceeds from the Father." In the Western church, centuries later, Frankish theologians introduced into their singing of the Creed the idea that the Holy Spirit "proceeds from the Father and the Son." The variation was tolerated by Rome, though not at first sung there...it was in fact disapproved of. Over the years, however, it became common in the West, and by the time of the schism it was apparently a common Western notion that the Orthodox had suppressed the words "and the Son."

Now this seems too fine a point to argue, in an age which has largely abandoned any belief in God; it's a bit like the angels-on-the-head-of-a-pin parody of scholastic disputation. However, the problem involved the nature of the Church itself. By what right, the Orthodox argued, did one bishop allow a change in a confession of faith which had been agreed upon by representatives of the whole Church?

There were continuing attempts at reuniting the Eastern and Western branches of the Church, the most notable of which was the Council of Florence (1438-9). But the Orthodox legates to that council returned home to find that their decisions were simply not supported by the people they thought they were representing: the claims of the papacy continued to be a stumbling block.

It is a battle in which neither side appears entirely virtuous. The part of Orthodoxy was frequently marred by a triumphal attitude towards Rome: now that the empire in the West had fallen, Rome should hand its laurels to Constantinople, the "new Rome". (That argument backfired on Constantinople after the Islamic conquests, when the newly powerful Russian Church argued that, with the fall of Constantinople, Moscow was "the third Rome.") The Roman side was equally unpleasant, concerned less with reconciliation than with submission. A low point was reached with the declaration of the Council of Florence that "Jews and schismatics" and others not in communion with Roman Catholicism were certainly damned.

Things are infinitely more charitable these days. Pope Paul VI and the late Patriarch Athenagoras of Constantinople have renounced the mutual excommunications of 1054. The problems remain — the Orthodox do not accept any ecumenical councils except the first seven, which included them, and the later Roman doctrines of papal infallibility and the Immaculate Conception are for this reason stumbling blocks. But there is a more cordial atmosphere now, and a willingness to face the past with more objectivity and less defensiveness.

The most obvious differences between Catholicism and Orthodoxy are structural. In Orthodoxy the local eucharistic congregation is understood to manifest the fullness of the Church; it is not a branch, but the whole body. The bishop is the center of the church, a sign of the continuity of the faith from apostolic times to the present, and of sacramental presence. (Patriarchs are not, as some Westerners think, Orthodox "popes"; nothing like papal power is claimed by any Orthodox bishop.) Bishops are chosen from the monastic clergy and, as monks, are celibate. Parish priests are usually married, though they must marry before ordination and may not marry again afterwards; perhaps because of this discipline laicization was, until quite recently, much more common in the Eastern

Orthodox than in the Catholic Church. The liturgy is repetitious and ornate, and is longer than most liturgical services in the West. Dogma is less precisely formulated than it is in Roman Catholicism. Unless precise formulation is considered absolutely necessary for reasons of worship or Church unity it is regarded as irreverent and legalistic; so there is, for example, no clear division between mortal and venial sin, and there is a reluctance to say that any sin can kill the life of grace in the soul. Similarly, while the Orthodox agree with Rome that there are seven sacraments they regard the number as a provisional thing, a convenient way of speaking about something which is finally mysterious. All of the sacraments (called "mysteries" in the Orthodox Church) are grace-bearing actions made possible by the presence of the Holy Spirit, but they are not necessarily limited to seven. Other actions of the Church are considered sacramental, even when they don't make the "official" list — the taking of monastic vows, for instance, or the consecration of a bishop. (This is very much like the flexible attitude of the early Church, which estimated the number of sacraments as two in some cases, eleven in others, and so forth—the blessing of holy water and exorcism were sometimes included, the main point being that the acts of the Church were human participations in divine activity.)

Another structural difference is in the comparative liberality of Orthodox canon law regarding marriage. While Orthodox theology regards marriage as a permanent sacrament, as Catholicism does, it also recognizes divorce, though penitential language is included in the ceremony for a second marriage. The general attitude is that there is no failing or sin which can't be forgiven, and nothing should keep people from participation in the sacraments. In other moral matters there is a latitude which might, in Lev Gillet's words, "astonish or even scandalize" some people. Gillet, an Orthodox monk, quotes a canon of St. Basil: "Fornication is not marriage; it is not even the beginning of marriage. That is why, if it is possible to induce those who have united themselves in fornication to separate, this is the best thing to do. But if they desire absolutely to live together, the penance reserved for fornication shall be imposed on them, yet without separating them, lest something worse should result" *(The Burning Bush,* Templegate, 1976). I don't know what that penance was, and Basil is hardly likely to win *Playboy's* "Bishop of the Year" award, but the tolerance, and the idea that there is "something worse", are interesting.

However, these structural variations between Orthodoxy and the West are not the primary differences, which stem instead from a basically different view of the Church and the Church authority, a different conception of original sin, and a consequent difference in spirituality and its aim.

Apart from the Holy Spirit, who dwells in the whole Church, there is no final authority or ultimately determinative doctrinal criterion in the Orthodox Church. The churches of the East, N. Zernov writes, "have always refused to identify Orthodoxy with any one teacher, system of theology, or institution...Orthodox theology, therefore, is experimental, rooted in Eucharistic worship, linked organically with prayers and asceticism, and consequently close to the heart and mind of all Christians. A sharp line of demarcation between trained theologians and lay people has never existed in the East. The Orthodox consider that the real distinction lies between those members of the Church who grow in holiness and wisdom, and those who remain absorbed in self, and are therefore incapable of sharing fully the life of grace offered to the faithful of the Christian community" *(Eastern Christendom,* Putnam, 1961).

The Orthodox writer John Meyendorff spells it out more precisely: "The Orthodox Church does not claim to possess any infallible or permanent criterion of truth or any monolithic structure: it sees unity in a communion of faith, of which the church itself — or rather the Holy Spirit always dwelling in the church — is the unique judge. The Spirit of Truth dwells in the communion of the faithful who are united by the bond of charity, and while he normally speaks through those who have the charism to teach, namely, the bishops, he belongs properly to the church as a Body. This Body is totally present everywhere the Eucharist is celebrated" *(The Orthodox Church,* Pantheon, 1962).

These statements by contemporary theologians don't sound much more advanced (though they are less ambiguous) than those of the Second Vatican Council on the priesthood of the laity and the principle of episcopal collegiality. However, the idea they express is not as new to Orthodoxy. When Pius IX suggested to the Orthodox bishops that Rome and the East had the same basic belief in ecclesiastical authority, they replied in a letter published in 1848, "Among us, neither Patriarch nor Councils could ever introduce new teaching, for the guardian of religion is the very body of the Church, that is the people *(laos)* itself." This idea has since been developed, particuarly among Russian theologians, into the idea of *sobornost,* "conciliarity," which places its emphasis on the responsibility of all believers for the fullness of faith. Even an ecumenical council cannot claim to be finally authoritative, according to this theory, until it is accepted by the people. While conservative Orthodox theologians find this a little too wild and democratic, the *sobornost* theorists have history on their side: The Second Council of Ephesus and the Council of Florence both met all criteria for ecumenical councils; the decisions of both were ultimately rejected by the Church. (This is true of Rome too: even though the decisions of the Council of Florence have never been formally repudiated, the teaching that all those who are not Roman Catholics will be damned has in fact been repudiated; Fr. Feeney was excommunicated for teaching it.)

Here again the Orthodox combination of conservatism and liberality shows itself. On the one hand there is the implicit belief that the truth must be accepted freely, or it cannot really be called the truth; on the other, it is the responsibility of every believer, whether bishop, priest, or layperson, to uphold the faith of the whole Church. Athanasius is frequently cited in this regard: alone among the bishops he fought against Arian definitions of Christian doctrine, and by refusing the consensus he finally won out against them.

This attitude can be a burden and a blessing, institutionally. It is a burden when it leads to stiff-necked beliefs in tradition. One early Eastern Bishop said in frustration, "The Lord said, 'I am Truth,' not 'I am custom.'" In Russia a simple change of ritual led to a schism because many believers could not make that distinction; the schismatic group — known as the "Old Believers" — exists to this day. But it is a blessing when it contributes (as it demonstrably does) to the survival of Christianity in times of persecution. During Russia's periodic anti-religious campaigns many of the strongest witnesses to Christianity have been laypeople who, unlike the clergy, have no livelihood to lose if they speak out, though in speaking out they may suffer. (Priests who have protested the treatment of Christians, Jews, and dissidents have been suspended.) Orthodox laypeople have been willing to criticize not only the government's policy towards religion; they have also criticized the compliant Orthodox hierarchy, without feeling that by doing so they are betraying Orthodoxy. It is precisely the defense of Orthodoxy, and their own responsibility for it, which leads them to take bishops to task.

Besides this different reading of Christian authority, Orthodoxy interprets the doctrine of original sin differently, and the interpretation leads to other differences. Here a couple of things should be mentioned. The first is that the Christian belief in a universal, all-encompassing fall is not an ancient Jewish belief, but is found first in Paul's writings. The second is that Paul's writings can be read more than one way. Augustine, who became the West's authority on the subject, believed that all humanity shared somehow in Adam's guilt. The darker interpretation of this belief continues in Calvinist theology, which speaks of humanity's "utter depravity." This was tempered in Catholic theology, but the belief that all shared in Adam's guilt continued. The view of the Eastern Fathers, however, was less dire than Augustine's. In their opinion the result of the fall was that all are born into a world radically estranged from its true nature. As part of that world we suffer the effects of that estrangement, and our sin is not the result of a personal share in Adam's guilt, but rather our presence in a fallen, mortal creation. "Death, on account of which all have sinned, has passed to all men," as Paul writes in Romans. Like members of an exiled royal family who are unaware of their real inheritance, or children who must be taught the liberties and responsibilities of adulthood, we must learn to accept and grow into our true nature.

This nature is the nature of the risen Christ, and it was revealed even before he died, on Mount Tabor where he was transfigured before Peter, James, and John. The Fathers of the Church speak of the "deification of man." Athanasius wrote, "The Word became man so that men might become gods." And St. Symeon wrote, "If God who was made man adopted me, a human being, and deified me, then I, a god by adoption, perceive Him who is God by nature."

The belief that human beings are in some sense meant to be what God is has appeared in the Western Church. You can find it in *The Cloud of Unknowing,* the writings of John of the Cross, Eckhart, and other mystics. In the West, however, it was peripheral to Church teaching, and sometimes it was considered heresy. In Orthodoxy it is central.

Deification does not mean that we deserve this gift. As Symeon writes, we are "gods *by adoption.*" Divine life is not something we can earn; it is the free offering of the only One who is divine by nature, a gift that shows the limitless nature of divine love. But in our present condition we can't accept it completely. First a change is demanded, repentance, and self-emptying. Our ordinary self-preoccupation, which we usually excuse by calling it "human nature," is in fact profoundly inhuman. "I will take away your hearts of stone and give you hearts of flesh," God says through the prophets. This self-emptying is the point of Orthodox spirituality, and it is also the point of the fasts which Orthodoxy keeps. (No specific sin-penalty is attached to those who do not fast; at Easter all are commanded to rejoice, "those who have fasted, and those who have not kept the fast." The Orthodox Church simply says that if you want to be a Christian, here is the way to begin.) The way to move out of ourselves towards God and our neighbor is through resisting our desires — and therefore our self-centeredness — and prayer. Metropolitan Anthony (Anthony Bloom) writes that this kind of spiritual and physical effort is "a time of joy because it is a time for coming home, a period when we can come back to life. It should be a time when we shake off all that is worn and dead in us in order to become able to live, and to live with all the vastness, all the depth and all the intensity to which we are called" *(Meditations,* Dimension Books, 1972).

Orthodox spirituality is practical — "experimental," as Zernov says — and it is centered in the ideal of constant prayer. The most common form this takes is the repetition of the "Jesus prayer," the repeated invocation "Lord Jesus Christ, Son of the Living God, have mercy on me." The Jesus prayer is increasingly popular in the West, as are the writings of Metropolitan Anthony, Lev Gillet, anthologies taken from the Orthodox classic the *Philokalia,* and other Orthodox works. This popularity might stem from the shallowness and the sterility of so much Western religious writing. The most influential Catholic writers — Thomas Merton, for example, and Henri Nouwen — have been profoundly affected by Orthodox spirituality. For the rest we have fundamentalism, or liberal theologies which equate Christianity with the latest therapy, or the most current political passion. One theologian even suggested a few years ago that what we really need is "a new concept of God."

Orthodox theology begins with the belief that God is unknowable. St. Gregory Nazianzus wrote that anyone who imagines that he knows God "has a depraved spirit," and he dealt sarcastically with over-academic approaches to theology: "You ask what is the procession of the Holy Spirit. Tell me first what is the unbegottenness of the Father, and I shall then explain to you the physiology of the generation of the Son and the procession of the Spirit; and we shall both of us be stricken with madness for prying into the mystery of God." Rather than ask questions about God, Christians should stand before the unknown God, worshipping in the spirit of the gospels (where instead of giving an answer to those who wanted to know where he lived, Jesus said, "Come and see"). The God we cannot reach by our own efforts reveals himself to the person who worships "in spirit and in truth." As we participate in this reality we are deified. Where in the West the marks of the stigmata were considered to be signs of God's life at work in the saint, the biographies of Orthodox saints tell stories of transfiguration, the faces of saints glowing so powerfully with "the uncreated light of Tabor" that their disciples could not bear to look at them. Transfiguration is frequently understood as a sign of the universal reconciliation which will occur at the end of time, when the whole universe will be brought to God, when in the words of Sergius Bulgakov, a Marxist convert to Orthodoxy, "the glorified state, inherent in the body of the risen Christ, will be communicated to the whole of creation."

How can Orthodoxy help the West? By restoring a sense of universal responsibility for Christianity, a spirit of contemplation which does not exclude action in and for the world, and a belief in tradition as a living and informative, rather than a restrictive, body of collective experience and reflection. We need a Christianity which can truly address the experience of modern men and women, while taking into account two important aspects of the modern condition. First, it is limited by a secular vision which is by and large opposed to tradition or, more subtly, regards itself as absolutely capable of evaluating tradition, as if for "modern man" a cloud had been lifted which covered the minds of human beings for millenia. Second, the modern world has seen genuine insights into the human condition, particularly in the socio-political, historical, and psychological disciplines; and the shortcomings of traditional answers are, partly because of these insights, much clearer to us than they were to our parents.

The result is a division between traditionalists whose appeals to past authority are ignored, and anti-traditionalists who reject that authority for individualistic interpretations of their condition; what else can they do, given the obvious fallibility of authorities which claimed to have absolute answers? The problem with this is that an exclusively individualistic attitude is almost inevitably too trusting of contemporary answers, answers which seem clearly right because they blend so easily into the environment which produced them. This transparency looks like truth, particularly when it is compared with tradition, which always appears incongruous because it carries its past on its back like a shell.

The Orthodox understanding of tradition, and of the responsibility of all believers for the faith of the community of believers, could restore a vital center to the West, saving it from authoritarianism on the one hand, and individualism on the other. Orthodox spirituality could restore to the West a spirit of contemplative prayer which has been lacking recently, a lack which may go a long way towards explaining the popularity of Pentecostalism and fundamentalist religion, with its stress on experience. Finally, too many Western approaches to asceticism have been negative, as if the flesh were evil. We could use a positive approach to fasting. And if it is asked why we should fast, apart from the reasons most frequently cited (it helps us to see our real limits rather than our imagined ones; by resisting our own wills we become more open to the will of God and the need of our neighbor) it should be enough to say that if Jesus felt the need to fast, we should not be easy about saying that we don't need to.

Until quite recently Orthodox and Western writers scored each other for the obvious differences between their traditions. Protestants found Orthodoxy too Catholic. Catholics deplored its lack of precision and what seemed at the time like a weak approach to Church authority. Orthodox criticized Catholics for making matters of faith out of opinion and for authoritarianism, while it criticized Protestantism for removing the Bible from the context of the Church, making it a kind of fossil. The whole West inclined towards cold legalism, Orthodox apologists claimed; and all sides ignored the saints who sprang up in every tradition, the ones who could see through to the Source.

With ecumenism a new humility has entered our relationship, and past institutional blindnesses are acknowledged. We see the inconsistencies of the past in a light which is objective, uncomfortable, but at least honest. Only a few diehards would defend Rome's authoritarianism. Protestants worry honestly about their own church identities. Orthodox theologians worry about Orthodoxy's abiding difficulty, which is nationalism.

Maybe by looking to the depths of our traditions, which once were one Church, we might discover the threefold unity which the Orthodox theologian Soloviev (who took communion in the Catholic as well as the Orthodox Church) saw in the vocations of Peter, Paul, and John. He believed that the divided Church now exercised those vocations separately. The Catholic Church exercised the unifying vocation of Peter. Protestantism maintained the uncompromising, scripture-centered fidelity which Paul brought to the early Church. Orthodoxy's emphasis was that of John: the Orthodox Church was the keeper of Christianity's interior life, a life which is the life of God. The celebration of a divine humanity could come as good news to a world which sets its sights so much lower.

The Trial of V. Poresh

Several years ago Vladimir Poresh was sentenced by a Soviet court to five years in a labor camp, followed by three years of internal exile. His official crime was "anti-Soviet agitation and propaganda." His actual offense was his membership in a remarkable group, the Christian Seminar.

The information we have about the Christian Seminar is based almost entirely on *samizdat* documents which have made their way West. What we know of the Christian Seminar and the fate of some of its members tells us a lot about the state of religion in the Soviet Union. It calls our own approach to Christianity into question as well.

The Christian Seminar is a group of young men and women, most of them converts to Christianity. The story of the group's founder, Alexander Ogorodnikov, is in many ways typical. Ogorodnikov was a cinematography student who grew disillusioned with Marxism and explored various forms of nihilism and the life of the hip subculture before Pasolini's film *The Gospel According to Matthew* led him to study Christianity. He joined the Orthodox church, lost his scholarship as a result of his conversion, and was given a job as a maintenance man at a tuberculosis clinic in Moscow and a shed—formerly a carpenter's workshop—to live in. It was there, in 1974, that the first meetings of the Christian Seminar took place.

Ogorodnikov gave the reasons for the Seminar's formation in a letter to Philip Potter, Secretary-General of the World Council of Churches: "We were convinced that our problems were being raised neither in church sermons, which are the only means for the religious education of believers, nor in the pages of the church journal, the *Journal of the Moscow Patriarchate,* which, moreover, is inaccessible to the ordinary Christian. Most important of all, in the Russian church the parish is not like a brotherly community where Christian love of one's neighbor becomes a reality. The State persecutes every manifestation of church life, except for the performance of a 'religious cult.' Our thirst for spiritual communion, religious education and missionary service runs up against all the might of the State's repressive machinery."

The Christian Seminar was an obvious outgrowth of the insight of the young Christians who gathered to form it: they knew that Christianity has a social resonance. They gathered in Ogorodnikov's shed to discuss the Bible and the Fathers of the Church, as well as the thought of Solovyov, Berdyayev, Bulgakov, Lossky, and other modern Orthodox thinkers. Members of the Seminar saw their work as threefold: they wanted to become theologicaly and philosophically grounded in a way which was closed to them under the officially tolerated church channels; they wanted to defend the rights of all believers to practice their religion; and they wanted to communicate with people of different faiths in and outside of the Soviet Unions. So they met for discussion and mutual support, produced two issues of a *samizdat* journal, *Obshchina* (Community), and wrote letters to fellow Christians in the USSR and abroad.

One Protestant member of the Seminar noted the willingness of the largely Orthodox group to learn from the Protestant experience, and the Seminar has made an effort to keep in touch with Christians in other countries, particularly with the Italian Catholic young organization "Communione e Liberazione." There is a strong ecumenical direction among members of the Seminar. They believe, for example, that the interaction of Russian Orthodoxy with Roman Catholicism will enable both churches to fulfill their vocations. (In this they have been influenced by Vladimir Solovyov, who believed that the Christian church must be at once Catholic in its pursuit of unity, Orthodox in its cultivation of the interior life and radical humility, and Protestant in its commitment to Biblical fidelity. Solovyov has been called a "Russian Newman" because he took communion in Catholic churches; but he felt that he had never left Orthodoxy, and the Orthodox claim him as their own. It may be that he was simply ahead of his time, and of our churches.)

The present condition of the Christian Seminar is difficult to know. Its founder, Alexander Ogorodnikov, is in prison; his sentence totals eleven years. At least eleven members have been arrested at various times. Only the second issue of *Obshchina* has reached the West. The first was confiscated by the KGB, and there may be no existing copies. The Seminar's meeting places have been raided, members have been beaten, and some of them, detained for "psychological disorders," have been forced to undergo damaging drug treatments. One member, Tatyana Shchipkova, was hounded out of a teaching job and in January of 1980 was sentenced to three years in a labor camp. The number of Seminar members now in prison is uncertain, but one of the cases about which we have some details is that of Vladimir Poresh.

Poresh was baptized in 1974. He contributed to *Obshchina* and was harassed and followed for a while. On August 1, 1979, Poresh was arrested and charged with anti-Soviet activities. Poresh conducted his own defense at the trial, which took place in Leningrad from April 23 to April 25, 1980.

"The indictment says I wanted to influence people," Poresh told the court. "Naturally I did: anyone who writes wants to influence and convince people. I have a negative attitude towards Soviet power but I have never called for struggle against it: fighting, struggling, poisoning the wells—nothing like that. My letter to A.I. Solzhenitsyn which features in this trial shows my conviction that the best way of struggling against Soviet power is not to struggle against it at all . . . I am talking primarily about spiritual action, about creating a new reality. So let me say once again that the aim of our journal, and my own personal aim, was the Christianization of the world, the liberation of people from social pressures: this is confirmed in my letter to Italian and French friends. At the preliminary inquiry I said that I had had meetings with two Italian girls, Agnesa and Graziella, from the Catholic youth organization 'Communione e Liberazione.' The program of this Catholic organization has been brought up at this trial. In it, translating from the Italian, one can read the following: 'We must struggle against social pressure and towards spiritual freedom.' If I had called for the restoration of capitalism (as has been stated here), then what would the Italians have to free themselves from, since they have freedom and democracy? Why in capitalist Italy do they have to struggle against society? The point is that we have one common goal: struggling against the social sinfulness of the world. We are calling for liberation from sin, from sinful life in society...I consider that our task is to create a Christian community transcending national boundaries, and a new Christian worldview.''

In his final statement to the court, Poresh said, ''The Procurator asked for a short sentence for me. I would have asked for a longer one, but I know that this would be too great an honor for me. There are people who have done much more for the church than I have.

''You have seen the witnesses. They are all my friends, believers and unbelievers. I saw joy on their faces: it was a joy to them to see me and a joy to me to see them. This hall was filled with a constant sense of joy in spite of the fact that I am in custody. Many of them helped me even though they did not completely share my convictions. This is a new religious community...This new spiritual reality, this communal Christian view of the world, is being created everywhere, even here in the courtroom, and here I see the goal and meaning of this trial.''

One understandable reaction to the story of the Christian Seminar is to feel some relief that few of us have suffered for our beliefs as Poresh and his companions have suffered, and we feel compassion for those who have been forced to endure such obvious injustice. But the more one reads of the struggles of those who suffer for their belief, the more another dimension of their belief, and ours, becomes apparent.

Most of us have never been forced to become aware of the cost of belief, or what it truly demands of us. They have been; and their words and witness have an intensity and hope which make most of what passes for Christianity in the West look pale and shallowly rooted. In a recent issue of *Sojourners* a visitor to Russia described a conversation with one Russian Christian, who said that he felt sorry for American Christians, because the materialism and ease of our society could so easily blind us to the demands of true Christianity. It is clear from the experience and testimony of those involved in the Christian Seminar that they understand something about Christianity which we would do well to learn: Christianity is not a seasoning with which we may choose to season our primarily secular experience. If it is real, it means thorough transformation.

Apart from telling something about these brave men and women this column has a twofold purpose. One is to acquaint *Commonweal* readers with the work of Keston College, a research center in England which publishes the excellent *Religion in Communist Lands.* All of the material quoted in this column appeared in several issues of that journal, which is objective, carefully researched, and indispensable for anyone who wants to learn about the condition of believers in Communist countries. The patrons of Keston College include leaders of the Protestant, Catholic, Orthodox, and Jewish communities of Great Britain, and articles in *Religion in Communist Lands* have dealt not only with Christianity and Judaism but also with the plight of Buddhist and Islamic believers. Keston College's address, for those who want to know more about its work, is Heathfield Road, Keston, Kent BR2 6BA, England.

The people who founded Keston College have also formed an organization to correspond with and aid Christian prisoners and their families. Aid to Russian Christians has an American branch. It is the Society of St. Stephen, R.R.#2, Box 51, Athens, Illinois 62613. The society needs money, and contributions are appreciated. But what it needs even more are individuals and groups willing to sponsor particular prisoners and their families. Since the cost of sending a package full of needed materials to the Soviet Union can be prohibitive, it makes sense for church groups, prayer groups, or other communities of Christians to do collectively what it might be difficult for someone to do individually. Write to the Society of St. Stephen for more information. The need is clear enough: there are nearly four hundred known Christian prisoners in the USSR, and their families share their fate. The wife of Father Gleb Yakunin, for example, is ill, unable to work, and depends upon the generosity of others to support her children.

The message which these Russian Christians bring to the West is revolutionary in the New Testament sense of the word. Toward the end of the transcript of Vladimir Poresh's trial, there is an interesting exchange.

"Poresh: Essentially I have been sentenced for my worldview. If our State is totalitarian, I am in fact breaking the law by having my own worldview, which I have never concealed and which I have talked about honestly and openly. I simply don't understand how I could have kept out of prison. What I did is a natural consequence of my convictions. According to the laws of our country I should have sat quietly, in silence; but it is not enough for a Christian to perform rituals: We can't stop there, we need the whole world.

"Judge: But you yourself stress that you were not persecuted for religious convictions. You were given the opportunity of being baptized and of baptizing your children. Even when you were in prison before the trial you had the opportunity to make your confession.

"Poresh: Yes, I had good relations at work, and even the Party organizer treated me properly and kindly. In prison they gave me a prayer book and a Bible. I am grateful for that. But this is not enough. We need the whole world.

"Judge: What? What do you need?

"Poresh: The whole world."

The Pluralism Puzzle

"There is no life without prayer," says the Russian philosopher Vasilii Rozanov. "Without prayer there is only madness and horror."

"That's your opinion; you're entitled to it," says our secular society.

The problem a believer faces is that belief has been made a subjective thing in a pluralistic society. Someone who tries to base his or her life on the conviction that we are called into being by what Dante called "the love which moves the sun and other stars" is faced with a system which necessarily regards this as one of many opinions, and can regard it as no more than that. Secularism has at one and the same time freed belief, and limited its shared meaning. Belief is no longer attached to respectability, or to political power, and this is as it should be. It is a good thing that the only good reason to be a believer today is because you believe. And this freedom has forced Christians to see the dark side of much Christian history. The dark side of the form of Christianity which allied itself with power was what happened to Jews and heretics and those whose politics or religion (sometimes the two were inextricably bound together) conflicted with the politics of the empire or the "Christian nation." Secularism was in part a reaction against religion's dark side, the equation of Christianity with citizenship, and it freed Christianity.

The most moving accounts of modern Christianity have come not from places of power but rather from places where power has been stripped from people, from poor nations where some Christians have thrown in their lot with the poor, or from Soviet labor camps where people suffer for their beliefs, or from Nazi concentration camps. In its loss of power this form of Christianity has learned something about what really sustains human beings. Where it attempts to gain power or to make good things happen through force it moves away from the possibility of this learning. Christianity's loss of power must not be seen as a punishment for past sins, as if good deeds would have been rewarded with more power, but as a part of the Christian vocation.

Although secularism has freed Christianity, it contains partially realized and as yet unrealized dangers. Secular humanism is a Promethean religion in which the human control of the universe and the ultimate value of human choice are affirmed as the highest goods. The affirmation of the importance of human freedom has been a good thing, and the Enlightenment ideal of the "rights of man" is one of the finest things which has happened to the human race. But secularism's anthropocentric idolatry and its assumption that spirituality is finally irrelevant are dangerous. A pluralistic society works very well, where day-to-day decisions are involved. The great problem of pluralism is that there are some absolutely essential questions with which pluralism cannot deal; or rather, in dealing with them it will impose the dark side of secularism.

Some of the most important questions we face cannot be answered within the only framework we have given ourselves for answering them, the legalistic and political one. These major questions involve our image of humanity: What is the human race for? What sort of creature, with what sort of destiny, is a human being? Questions of this sort are usually considered to be politically irrelevant, in that they involve matters which we have agreed to leave out of the democratic political process. The Ayatollah has very clear and definite answers to those questions, and we do not envy Iran. The problem is that some of our most important public problems do involve the way we regard these questions, and the decisions which are made about them reflect systems of belief, whether those beliefs are explicitly acknowledged or not.

A couple of cases in point are the debates over capital punishment and abortion. Contrary to the claims of many pro-lifers, abortion is a profoundly religious issue. They are right to argue that it is not a denominational one, though denominations obviously have a place in the debate. (Catholics tend to be pro-life; Unitarians tend to be pro-choice.) I have pointed out elsewhere that it comes down to the question of where you believe human value comes from. If it is intrinsic, if human life is important simply by virtue of the fact that it exists, you imply that value is given. It is there, whatever anyone thinks of it. But if life's value is not given solely by human beings, it has an other-than-human source. A given value implies a giver—a divine one. If on the other hand you believe that values are a human symptom, then the value of a human life depends upon its being welcomed by the human community; if you believe that human beings are the ultimate source of value and valuing, then the morality of abortion or capital punishment shifts. It does make sense to say that whether or not the life in the womb is human, it is not a person in any interesting sense of the word until it is the sort of being to whom others can meaningfully relate. If there is no divine giver of value, if what matters ultimately is the way we regard one another and all value is to be found in that mutual regarding, the pro-choice position makes absolutely good sense. This latter point of view is a secular one and cannot be accepted by believers, just as the belief that values have a more than human source cannot finally be accepted by secular people.

I do not mean to imply that we are all consistent here. Many opponents of abortion are advocates of capital punishment, and many proponents of abortion on demand are opposed to the death penalty. The social attitudes of believers are not, unfortunately, always consistent with their beliefs; the same thing is true, fortunately, of secular humanists. What is important here is to see that what we believe about the nature of human life does in fact have a social importance.

At the international level there is a similar problem. The future of the human race has been tied to the nation-state in an obscene way. In order to insure the survival of particular governments and ideologies, we have given ourselves the ability to destroy every human life. Today's mood has been compared to the mood of Europe during the time of the bubonic plague; but there is an added insanity here, as if Damocles were holding the sword by a thread over his own head. Here the problem is that we have no clear sense of human sacredness, and even the best secular ideas are violated. We are building a very fragile bridge across a chasm which may not have a far side. The only apparent value is that whoever has power now has assumed the right to do absolutely anything to hold onto it.

The problem believers face is that where solutions are imposed in a pluralistic society they are likely to be imposed with a bias towards secularism. One way to oppose this is, of course, to meet power with power. But it might be more effective to reveal, as much as possible, the religious nature of secular humanism, and the ways in which our values form our approaches to social questions. Religious and philosophical questions are, at some crucial points, central to political considerations. They are whether we like that fact or not. The denial of this reality reminds me of a wonderful line from the movie *Atlantic City*. An empty-headed young woman is talking about her view of life. "I don't believe in gravity," she says.

Loving God for Nothing

Familiarity may breed contempt, but it breeds something even more dangerous where religion is concerned. It may lead us to think that we know what we are talking about. I don't mean that laymen may be seduced into thinking that they know what only qualified theologians *really* know; it is at least as much a danger to the theologian as it is to the layman. Religious language can become so interesting that we forget what it is for, or so familiar that we imagine we know. We forget how strange it would be to hear the words of the Gospel fresh. We become comfortable with language which is meant to move us away from what we regard as comfort; we are secure and at home with a message which leaves us with nothing to be secure about, and invites us to a way of life in which security, as a pursuit, must be left behind.

Each Sunday along with a church full of other people I recite a creed in which I say that God became human. We say it easily, half paying attention. We affirm belief in a God none of us can possibly imagine, and say that this unknowable one became a human being, which is to say that someone unimaginable became a sort of creature we do not understand. Does any of us know what a human being is? Irenaeus said that the glory of God is man, fully realized. What would that be like? I am not sure that we have the equipment to recognize a fully realized human being.

The words of the creed inspire hope. They move us at obscure levels. They encourage us to believe a number of things: that lives which involve suffering and joy are not without meaning, and this meaning is somehow rooted in the compassion of God—whatever God may be, whatever we are.

But even these hopes and the need for meaning rise like bubbles in a kind of mental soup which boils constantly without our being aware of it. We are not aware enough of consciousness itself, or how it works, or the ways in which ego can use religion and religious language to shore itself up and protect itself from the implications of the words we use too easily.

Thomas Merton's fascination with Buddhism was not, as some conservatives have suggested, a decadent turn taken by a rebellious monk. It was rather the discovery of something central to the life of prayer. Buddhism looks without either hope or despair, and certainly without sentimentality, at the phenomenon of awareness itself, and in the process it deals with problems which have everything to do with spirituality. At the beginning of *Cutting Through Spiritual Materialism* (Shambhala) Chögyam Trungpa, a Tibetan Buddhist now working from Boulder's Naropa Institute, writes, "We have come here to learn about spirituality. I trust the genuine quality of this search but we must question its nature. The problem is that ego can convert anything to its own use, even spirituality. Ego is constantly trying to acquire and apply the teachings of spirituality for its own benefit . . . In order to reassure ourselves, we work to fit into our intellectual scheme every aspect of our lives which might be confusing. And our effort is so serious and solemn, so straightforward and sincere, that it is difficult to be suspicious of it." The desire to possess the right kind of spirituality, he suggests, can be every bit as materialistic as the desire to own a car or a new refrigerator.

Similar approaches to spirituality can be found in the West. The anonymous author of *The Cloud of Unknowing* says that the most pious and holy thoughts are dangerous distractions at a certain point, and he encourages a deliberate forgetting, and a knowledge that God is unknowable "except by love.'' St. Basil said that anyone who claimed to know God was depraved, and Meister Eckhart wrote of the Godhead beyond God. He describes something which comes startlingly close to the Buddhist ideal: ''The just man loves God for nothing, neither for this nor for that, and if God gave him wisdom or anything else he had to give, except himself, the just man would not look at it, nor would it be to his taste; for he wants nothing, seeks nothing, and has no reason for doing anything. As God, having no motives, acts without them, so the just man acts without motives. As life lives on for its own sake, needing no reason for being, so the just man has no reason for doing what he does'' (*Meister Eckhart,* translated by R.P. Blakney, Harper).

Merton was aware that this could be found in Western spirituality, but was unafraid of the East's direct approach. It is a directness which we need desperately. Religion can be another form of noise, joining politics and psychology and television and best-sellers in the swarm of distractions we present ourselves with constantly.

The most basic question is, who is it that sits down to pray? What is it in us that scripture addresses when we are told to leave everything to follow Christ? What is it in us that is transformed, or is even capable of being transformed? There is only one way to find out: you sit down, try to be quiet (which means quieting the body as well as the mind) and concentrate on a few words—a short prayer, a line from one of the psalms. Within a few minutes you are thinking of a hamburger, or something that needs to be done, or a conversation you might be having with someone. You bring the mind back, and within seconds it's gone again. If you are tired you may find youself close to dreaming. It doesn't help to be terribly strenuous in fighting these distractions; in a way they serve a valuable function: they show you what really leads you through a day, what you really care about, what you are and are not. What you are not matters deeply: the process of trying to pray can reveal how empty and cold-hearted we really are. We have the desire to love, coupled with a complete inability to do so, and at the same time our greatest passion may be buried resentment or anger. This isn't meant to discourage us; it is a mercy to see it, to know our emptiness and our need. We are driven by it and led around by it, until we can see it. In Ezekiel God says, "I will take away your hearts of stone and give you hearts of flesh." But before this can happen we have to know how stony-hearted we are, or else we will simply admire the poetry of Ezekiel, which is not what Ezekiel is for.

Any spirituality must, in the Quaker phrase, "speak to our condition" to be genuinely helpful, but it is easy to be distracted from learning what that condition is. What we are is not necessarily what we think we are; it is certainly not simply the sum of our feelings and aspirations. What is called for is an intense listening, a stillness in the face of our feelings. We ordinarily react to them; it is important instead to pay attention to them without being led by them.

Take the rather common experience of feeling misunderstood, or of being offended somehow. We can resent our situation and insist on our righteousness or on our innocence. Or we can explore what it is in us that is wounded. What do we lose, or think we will lose, if we are not seen precisely as we would like to be seen? We are trying to keep in place a picture of the self which serves not only as a self-portrait (and a flattering one at that) but also as a shield. When it is attacked it matters more than anything in the world that we hold on to it and keep it from being damaged. Why? Can't we live without it?

At one age we need a self-image which can be shamed into decent behavior or encouraged by praise. We would not be bearable company if in our coming to maturity we had not been civilized by a system of goads and rewards. But at another stage it may be crucial to let go of the picture, or to get out of the armor; it may be an impediment to spiritual growth. Here the danger is in replacing one suit of armor with another, more subtly designed: the need to make spiritual progress and to know that we are doing so can, in Chögyam Trungpa's words, be a form of "spiritual materialism" which is every bit as crass as the desire to own a new car. But it is made to seem less worldly by the ego, because it is "spiritual." The desire to be perceived by others or, more insidiously, to perceive ourselves as holy, or good, or wise, is as limiting and foolish as the desire to be thought sexually attractive or financially powerful. Our attachment to any of these things, including any need I might feel to be right about what I am writing this minute, has to be seen for what it is: the ego's way of holding on to us, to protect itself. It isn't that right or wrong do not matter; but any attachment I have to the need to be right has nothing at all to do with my love for the truth.

There are many problems and controversies which properly concern us. They include the church's role in social transformation, the role of women in the church, lay ministries, and there are many others. But above all each of us must try to be clear about prayer. We need a spirituality in which the daily conditions of marriage, family, friendship, work, and social struggle become a school of spirituality. This could seem to be a recommendation of individualistic soul-polishing and a turning away from communal concerns. It isn't; we can't wait until all of our motives are clear before we do anything. But the social implications of Christianity are addressed frequently these days, and our radical need for a living spirituality is not.

There has been a lot written and said about the church's current "state of crisis," and at the level of church politics there is something to the notion. But the most vital crisis is one which has been with the church since its beginning: it is learning to hear the words of the Gospel as pointed and personal, aimed at the heart. We must recover the strangeness of their original proclamation. What is it in us that Jesus addresses when he says that we must lose our lives in order to find them? Eckhart said, "To get at the core of God at his greatest, one must first get into the core of himself at his least, for no one can know God who has first not known himself. Go to the depths of the soul, the secret place of the Most High, to the roots, to the heights; for all that God can do is focused there."

The Sea Frozen Inside Us

There is a fascinating problem with traditional religions. They can serve as challenges to every dimension of our life, as agents of transformation; or they can reassure us that we do not have to change at all. They can stand in the way of transformation. A revelation, a vision which was meant to break through our ordinary perceptions in order to free us becomes instead a comfortable and familiar part of an old landscape, or a piece of our soul's furniture, something like the accustomed feeling of a bannister we touch every night on our way up to bed: it is a comfort to know that whatever else happens in our life, this at least will remain the same. This is so persistent a temptation that for some people it is a religion's main use, its reason for being.

Kafka wrote a letter once in which he said something which applies to religion as well as to literature: "If the book we are reading does not wake us, as with a fist hammering on our skull, why then do we read it? So that it shall make us happy? Good God, we would also be happy if we had no books, and such books as make us happy we could, if need be, write ourselves. But what we must have are those books which come upon us like ill-fortune, and distress us deeply, like the death of one we love better than ourselves, like suicide. A book must be an ice-ax to break the sea frozen inside us."

It may seem strange to compare this to the Gospel, which means "good news," when Kafka speaks of ill-fortune and distress. The Gospel speaks of life, and he speaks of death and suicide. But the good news of the Gospel is not cheery, and the life involved is a life so directly related to death that we place the cross at the center of our places of worship. There can be no resurrection without it. I am uncomfortable writing this, because we have a way of talking easily of what death (not to speak of life) means, as if from our vantage point we had clarity about these things. As Kafka said, we are frozen inside. We may boil with feeling, but it is a feeling remarkably unrelated to the real situation of any human being outside ourselves, and is only related to our own situation in a confused and murky way.

Ordinarily we feel another's pain only by a kind of analogy: I would hate to be in that position (whatever it is), and try to imagine it. Seldom does the misfortune of another strike us as a misfortune which we suffer ourselves. When we allow another's misfortune to affect our life in any way, we think of this as a moral luxury. Isn't it decent of us to behave compassionately? (We could, after all, have chosen not to.) We regard compassionate action as a matter of choice, something done "from the goodness of our hearts," and admire those who are tirelessly compassionate, as if they were only doing more frequently, and with more energy, what we sometimes do ourselves.

But in regarding compassion this way we are more sealed into ourselves than we were when we were unreflectively selfish. Francis of Assisi said that God led him to lepers, who had previously repelled him, and he "entered into the pain of their hearts." Most of what we consider compassion is not only *not* like that, but contains an element of removal which makes entering the pain of another absolutely impossible. This removal involves an element of satisfaction or gratitude that we are not ourselves suffering as the other does; it is a form of psychic self-protection. It is a self-protection which collapses sometimes, when someone we love deeply suffers. The agony of someone we love *helplessly*, as we love our children, pierces us; it is something we feel in our hearts, and it may be that it is important to us spiritually in direct proportion to our helplessness before it. The love which is not a matter of choice but a condition of our being, the love we cannot help, which ties us—however we *feel* about it—to another, is most like God's love, or the love Saint Francis was led to.

We put so much stock in feelings, as if it were primarily through feeling that we could come to understand the world. To question this idea, or to doubt that in some significant way we are the sum of our feelings, is nearly heretical.

Christianity is currently associated with states of mind, convictions, proper as opposed to improper emotions; or it is considered an institutional allegiance, or a heritage to which one ought to be loyal; or it is considered a system of ideas. As something which demands a thorough transformation of everything in us, everything we are, it is invisible.

Our ordinary understanding of Christianity has everything to do with the Enlightenment reduction of religion to the realm of the subjective. Its validity is seen as dependent on the depth of the emotions it arouses, or the tenacity (if not the depth) of our emotional commitment to it. I do not want to return to a world in which Christianity was as taken for granted as we take the law of gravity, if there ever was such a relaxed version of Christendom. Unless the Gospel comes to us fresh, as real news, what we receive is not the Gospel but a story which uses the same words, characters, and descriptions of events to *turn the Gospel into its opposite*: it becomes a reassurance that nothing really has to change, as long as we obey the rules and don't stray too far ethically. But one of the few good things about the world of established Christendom was that Christianity was seen as something so much more real than emotional or psychological response, so much more like the moon or the sun, that even those celestial symbols were less important than trinitarian and angelic ones. This understanding made it clear that our emotions are at best the psychic shadows of real spiritual events.

In a discussion of the Lord's prayer in his excellent book *Living Prayer* (Templegate, 1966) Metropolitan Anthony Bloom says that to pray "deliver us from the evil one" requires "such a reassessment of values and such a new attitude that we can hardly begin to say it otherwise than in a cry, which is as yet unsubstantiated by an inner change in us. We feel a longing

116

which is not yet capable of achievement; to ask God to change us in the trial is to ask for a radical change in our situation." Later in the same chapter Bloom says that one of our dangers is the fact that "when we realize that we can no longer depend upon all that we are accustomed to find reliable around us, we are not yet ready to renounce those things." He speaks of the need to acknowledge this fact at its deepest point, where "despair has led us to faith," and emphasizes the importance of making sure that we do not despair of final victory but rather "of the means we have used to reach it."

What does all of this have to do with traditional religion? I am afraid that for most of us—priests, laypeople, religious—the churches serve too often as means of reinforcing emotions we do not want to see challenged in any basic way. When Jesus encountered people their response was either defensive, or one which involved an awakening—in Kafka's terms, a thaw. The presence of Jesus transformed everything.

We are not comfortable (and there is no way to be comfortable with this idea) with the knowledge that, if Christianity is true, it changes everything. Because this causes discomfort, it becomes necessary to make Christianity more comfortable, to tell the same story in a way which reverses its moral, rather than succumb to a discomfort, a despair, and a distress with the means of self-protection we have developed to keep us from being changed. But to feel that distress is the beginning of change, and is necessary.

Our approach to religion and religious education now aims too often at arousing appropriate feelings in us, in the hope that the feeling will lead the feeler to something deeper and more substantial. Sometimes the feelings, particularly the most powerful ones, are seen as proof that we are on the right track. This is precisely the wrong way to go. Liturgy, spiritual direction, and the other guides we have ought to make more profound demands on us. They should not take our feelings for granted as good things, but ought to force us to question our feelings as deeply as we ought to question our thoughts. Everything about us needs transformation. There is no better proof of that than the ordinary state of ordinary Christians.

We claim to believe that there is someone who loves us so deeply that he died to show us the depths of that love, and because of that love offers us a life which we cannot imagine. Our distractions are so thick, our sleep so profound, that it took his death just to get our attention. On the whole we remain relatively unmoved by this fact. The gnostics compared our ordinary state of mind to sleep, to dreaming, to drunkenness. They may have been heretical in some ways, but certainly not here.

The Last Solitude

During Holy Week this year I thought—not surprisingly, I guess—about death. Traditional religions have been accused of making us all conscious of our guilts, of playing on our fears of death and what may follow death. And it is true that no religion ignores this dreadful subject; all great traditions deal with death in a way which is closer to a stammer than to clarity. What they have in common is something we take so much for granted that we may not see how odd it is for human beings from all of the major religious traditions to share this one perception: the way we live has something to do with how we die, with what death will mean for us.

Secularists—which is to say, most people in their ordinary ways of viewing these things, whether they are consciously secularist or not—exhibit a different attitude. It is hard to speak simply about it because there is no secular church, no common voice or authority which can say what matters from a secular point of view. But the attitude in the air, the sensibility that reflects the assumptions which drive the age (this sensibility can't almost by definition, be as clearly articulated as belief), is that death is an interruption, an accident, something which must be postponed and avoided and challenged wherever it can be. As something which reveals us as we truly are it works only insofar as it shows the bravery of, for example, the terminal cancer victim or the person who has the time to display courage before the assembled family.

That death itself might have a significance beyond the one which offers the dying person a setting in which to die dramatically, interestingly, heroically—this is not part of the way we ordinarily regard the one thing which all of us can count on. Secularism has decided that what we have come to call "this life" is the only one which matters; and the reason is that it is really the only life which exists at all. Death itself is a blank, a backdrop against which the important drama is acted. Death can tell us nothing about life, except by way of reaction.

There is something unavoidably blank about death. None of us has been there; none of us can say what it is like. I discount the stories told by people who have seen the tunnel of light and all that; there has been enough oxygen left in their brain cells to allow them to experience such sensations. In fact no one with a straight line on the EEG has come back to say anything at all.

Most Christians and most more or less secular people who cherish some idea of an afterlife make an identification of the mind—that is, the part of us that has memories and tastes, affections and aversions—with the soul, the part that is supposed to hang around somewhere after the body is gone. The ancient division of the human being into a three-part rather than a two-part reality (aside from it appealing to Christians) was probably closer to whatever may turn out to be the case. In shoving "mind" and "spirit" into the same category we have created some real problems. But when we don't, we face a scary mystery. That is probably the better place for us to be.

If I assume that whatever survives my death will be a sort of me-without-a-body (an entity which doesn't sweat or need haircuts or have problems with flatulence but which does remember how nice the sun felt one day in July or how noble the causes I cared about were), if I think that whatever I will be after I am dead has much to do with what I think of now as "me," I am, among other things, ignoring some very impressive evidence. One bunch of evidence comes from science. That may be enough to descredit it with fundamentalists, but not with me.

Strokes can cancel out a lot of what we think of as the self. Brain damage does to those memories what electrical surges do to information in a computer, and to ask "where did that information go?" may properly be answered "nowhere." It may be possible to think of a kind of heavenly account where all those earthly cancellations wind up, bit by bit, until the heart's stopping tosses the balance over the wall into whatever stores all that stuff on the other side. I would hate for Christians to have to depend on this sort of thinking to shore up their belief, though. It doesn't do a thing for mine.

For years now various Christian theologians have been trying to point out the fact that the New Testament does not tell us to believe in something as abstract and finally indefinable as "the immortality of the soul." Instead, it says that Christ is risen, and this tells us something about what we will be. What it tells us is less precise than we would like, and this has led fundamentalists to search Scripture in their usual unimaginative way for descriptions of the length of heaven and the kinds of clothes we will get to wear, leading to pictures which make what happens to us after death look like a visit to a particularly boring sort of theme park. Preachers who rely on this tactic should be warned; I have met people who have left behind all ideas of eternal life because of their fear that it will be in some way "more of the same"—more of this life, even if it is this life clothed in white robes and walking on streets of gold, which, after all, would get boring after about five minutes.

But people who think that they have gone beyond this and talk instead about "heightened experiences" or somthing of that sort should realize that they are doing more of the same sort of thing, with California accents. What death means is what it seems to mean: an ultimate cancellation of everything we thought we were about, the end of everything we want to hold on to, whether white robes or profound experiences.

The responses we make to this absolute blank reveal a lot. The secular answer reveals the secular belief that life is what we know it to be, even granted the fact that we may be surprised by our capacities; and this is why stories of courage and displays of good character in the face of extinction are so moving from the secular point of view (and from any other point of view, for that matter). Buddhism answers with a questioning of our desire to hold on to particular images of the self, making of the self a solid and subsistent thing, and therefore dooming us to tragedy. Once we know that this is an illusion, our grasping will not anchor us to an inevitably tragic destiny; but this knowledge must be a transforming thing, not merely an intellectual acknowledgment. Judaism offers us the example of Job, and the paradox of a God who answers Job's anguished questions with still more questions—questions which really are better than Job's, and are probably the most majestic and wonderful example in history of putting someone in his place. God's answer to Job includes a rebuke to Job's comforters, who are accused of not being quite honest. (We need more of that.)

Where the religious response to death differs from the secular response is in the religious assumption that what we regard as life is only a part of our reality. Secularism stresses what we can know: this is *our* triumph. If the presence of death underscores that knowledge, it stretches our present awareness, and for that reason is profoundly important.

Religious traditions can't settle for this. Death not only tells us what we are moving towards, or what the backdrop is; death, from a religious point of view, is part of the definition. Buddhism suggests that the fear of death is part of a complex web of understandings which are themselves part of the problem—including our attraction to the idea that a noble death is impressive. What does that death preserve? If we hope that it preserves something we are on the wrong track; if we think that death dissolves something we are also on the wrong track, since there is really not a single thing, a subsistent entity, which goes through the process of dying. Judaism preserves the mystery of the source of our being here without answering any of our questions about it. That is certainly important both to the Jewish opposition to idolatry and to the connection Christians need to make between the Judaism we come from and the doctrines we speak about too easily. In the case of two very different traditions, Buddhism and Judaism, death tells something about the nature of our relationship with a universe which is ordered in ways we are not capable of comprehending.

Is it possible to believe that Jesus is risen, that Christ is Lord, and also take to heart the unknowing which must form any true and non-idolatrous response to death? If our response is designed simply to comfort us, to serve as a security blanket against the inevitable cancellation we'd rather not think about, it isn't any more worthy of adults than belief in Santa Claus. To the extent that religion is part of filling that need it deserves all the cynicism atheists bring to it.

When Jesus approached Lazarus's tomb, he wept. At the garden of Gethsemane, needing human companionship, he found himself alone before God (a radical solitude which would have been there even if his friends had found it possible to stay awake) and, according to Scripture, "his soul was filled with dismay and dread." He asked that the horror would be lifted from him. It wasn't. His prayers, from the only point of view we can possibly understand, were answered with silence.

I find this much more helpful than all of the stuff which would reconcile me to the fact that someday I may die before the people I love do, or they may die before I do, and some of us will be left feeling torn open. There is no Christian doctrine which says we have to feel good about what life deals us. What we are told is that "we are God's children now; it does not yet appear what we shall be, but we know that when he appears we shall be like him, for we shall see him as he is" (1 John 3:2). We have hope through being baptized into that life, and have no right to any information beyond the staggering news we have been shown in Jesus' Resurrection.

The comparisons which are made between growing plants, children in the mother's womb, things growing in the dark waiting still to be revealed—all of this has to do with the nature of our present consciousness. It is impossible for us to know what the cancellations involved in death and suffering mean in any but the most tentative and awkward ways. All we know is that they cause us pain. We have, after that, Jesus appearing as a stranger to the desciples walking towards Emmaus, known to them in the breaking of the bread.

There is an irreverence involved in trying to imagine much more than this. Imagining isn't the point, rather it is the more sober and infinitely more hope-filled work of trying to receive everything that we have been given.